STARTING A
SMALL BUSINESS

BUSINESS GUIDEBOOKS

SELF-HELP GUIDES FOR SMALL BUSINESSMEN

STARTING A SMALL BUSINESS

ALAN & DEBORAH FOWLER

SERIES FOREWORD BY DAVID TRIPPIER,
UNDER SECRETARY OF STATE AT THE
DEPARTMENT OF INDUSTRY

Sphere Reference

Sphere Study Aids
30/32 Gray's Inn Road
London
WC1X 8JL

First Published 1983
Reprinted 1985, 1986

Phototypesetting by
C. Leggett & Son Ltd., Mill Green Road, Mitcham,
Surrey.

Printed and bound in Great Britain by
Cox & Wyman Ltd., Reading, Berks.

CONTENTS

SERIES FOREWORD

by David Trippier MP,
Parliamentary Under Secretary of State for Industry

The environment for small businesses has changed for the better in the past four years. An effective Loan Guarantee Scheme and generous tax relief through the Business Expansion Scheme are only two of many in over 100 Government measures to provide incentives and remove obstacles to business enterprise. Our efforts are complemented by a welcome improvement in attitudes in commerce and industry towards the small business operator.

Vital though these changes are, the success of any new expanding business will always depend on the skill, knowledge and tenacity of those running the firm. Practical sources of expertise and advice, as provided by this series of Business Guidebooks, are invaluable aids for the busy entrepreneur. General business management and finance, without doubt, cause the most problems and biggest headaches for the small firm.

Certainly many young businesses have been given a better chance of success by the increasing availability of help with the particular challenges that beset them. I am encouraged by figures which show for the two years, 1981 and 1982, 'births' of new firms well in excess of 'deaths' in spite of the worldwide economic recession.

A flourishing small firms sector in any national economy brings new energy, new enterprise and new initiatives into industry and commerce. These attributes have never been more necessary than in today's tough economic climate and highly competitive world markets. To this end, these Business Guidebooks will be a worthwhile investment for every new and expanding business.

INTRODUCTION

One cold grey evening when my business looked as though it had failed and everything seemed hopeless, I met an old friend at my parents' house.

He listened very attentively to my tale of woe. The story of the last six years — building a business from nothing, the hours of slog, success beyond my wildest dreams and now in a few short weeks it looked as though it was all over.

His response has always given me comfort — he said 'What happens now doesn't matter, what is important is that you did it. It would have been far more terrible not to have done it at all.'

It is an over simplification but the gist of what he said is true. How many times have you listened to someone else's success story and thought, 'I could have done that — I could have done *better* than that.' Somehow though, these thoughts normally remain a pipe dream. We all have such varied and diverse abilities, yet we shy away from exploiting them.

The object of this book is to try and persuade you 'to have a go' — to start your own business. Perhaps you are unemployed or under-employed, unhappy and unfulfilled in your job. Perhaps you are a woman contemplating your children starting school and time on your hands for the first time in years. Perhaps you are retired but not content to give up work yet. Or perhaps it is simply that there is something you have always wanted to do and have never quite had the courage to try.

We are by definition 'A nation of shop keepers'. We are a funny island race with enormous regional variations, but from Caithness to Cornwall it is a fact that we are better fulfilled and better motivated by direct involvement. In big companies so often one loses a sense of identity and purpose — it is difficult to feel useful, to feel that one is making a contribution. Your own business will be tough going but you will find hidden resources you did not know you had.

Alan and I have had our successes and failures but we do have between us vast experience in starting and building a business. This book is divided into four sections. It deals with the trials and tribulations, from taking the decision right through to coping with tremendous success or failure. Most chapters include case histories — real life experiences of other people's fight to build a business. This is not a text book — we are simply aiming to help you take the first shaky steps — and pointing out some of the joys and sorrow along the way.

If by the time you have reached the end of this book you have decided to go ahead, then all we can offer you is our own basic philosophy — if you want to achieve something badly enough, you usually succeed.

Good luck.

DEBORAH FOWLER.

'TO DOUGLAS M — THANK YOU FOR YOUR HELP,
YOUR PATIENCE AND FOR SETTING SUCH A
SPLENDID EXAMPLE.'

Credits

We have had an enormous amount of help
and advice in the preparation of this book.
We would like particularly to thank:

Stephen Adamson
Barclays Bank
Alfred Danzig
Douglas Hamilton
David Harris
Hotchkiss Kruger Associates
Lady Joseph
Mai Sim Lai
Stanley Lee
Viola Niness
David Peters
Bill Rivers
John Runacres
Stephen Saye
Williams & Glyn's Bank
. . . and, of course, all our case histories.

'The Decision'

The first section of this book asks you to stand back and consider whether you are really making the right decision in starting your own business. You are probably thinking — 'How irritating. I wouldn't have bought this book in the first place if I hadn't already decided to go ahead.'

Agreed, but just do us, and yourself, a favour. Before you skip straight to Section Two, and get down to the meat of the problem, read through 'The Decision'.

Although at the moment every encouragement is being given to people to start their own businesses, *it is not easy*. Far more new ventures fail than suceed. There comes a point where the odds are just too highly stacked against success.

Do not misunderstand us. In this book we will be trying to persuade you to have a go. But you do need to start in the right way, with the right attitude of mind, and in the right circumstances.

Sorry, if this sounds like a sermon but bear with us and read on. All we want is for you to succeed.

1. Attitude of mind — are you a single minded workaholic with an over-developed sense of your own importance?

Our chapter heading sounds gruesome, doesn't it?

On face value, it appears we are suggesting that to start your own business you have to give up all idea of ever having a holiday again, and as if that were not enough, you need to be impossibly pompous as well!

Is that what we are saying? Well, yes . . . and no!

Let us look at the question of workload first. Except in very rare instances, if you wish to start your own business you should expect and accept that for the first few months and in some cases, years, you will be working most of every waking hour. Probably it will be a seven days a week job and when you are not actually working, you will be worrying about it.

There is so much to do. Just marshalling your product or service into a saleable state is no easy task. Then you have to go out and find your market and persuade that market to accept what you have to offer. Then there is the question of finding the money and setting up all the legalities and administration to run your business.

All this has to be achieved in the first two or three months of trading if your business is to succeed at all.

In our family we always refer to any one starting out in business as having the '3 a.m. syndrome'. To explain, I (in this case, Deborah) started a business ten years ago selling children's clothes by mail order. I had no capital and so could afford to employ no one. I produced a little catalogue and placed a few advertisements and sat back. As the orders came in I cut out the cloth and made up the garments. Within a few days I was sitting up until 3 a.m. cutting and sewing. 'This cannot go on,' I thought, so after a week I employed two seamstresses and concentrated on cutting out. Within days I was cutting out until 3 a.m.! 'This will not do,' I thought, so I bought a cutting machine. Yes, you have got the picture — I was soon back to 3 a.m. again! If your business starts to take off in any significant way — indeed if it is to work at all — then you have been warned. It has to be 'graft' all the way . . . hopefully to the bank!

'An over-developed sense of your own importance' may sound a bit strong but really it is not. It is very important that before you start your business, you seek as much advice as possible and that having made the decision to go ahead, the process of learning does not stop there. Having said that, however, you need to build up within yourself a hard core of confidence and commitment to what you are doing. You cannot please all the people all the time and you are going to suffer your fair share of critics.

When friends are critical on a personal level, we are usually able to cope — we tell ourselves they have misunderstood the facts, are jealous of us, or whatever. It is not so easy, however, when people start criticising your business aspirations. You will find you have much less confidence. Perhaps, you think, they can see the wood for the trees, see something you cannot. Stuff and nonsense. You have a goal, stick to it. Mind your own business and tell them to mind theirs.

In each of the chapters in this first section of the book we will be helping you to determine whether you are a suitable candidate for starting your own business. You are your own best judge and jury. Regardless of how many other people's advice you seek, 'The Decision' can only, and should only, be taken by you.

So here is the message for this first chapter — you have got to be able to work like a beaver, have the commitment of believing in what you are doing and the strength of character to fight for those beliefs in the teeth of opposition. To start your own business, you have got to have a strong stomach. The ultimate responsibility is yours and yours alone — can YOU bear that burden?

Case History No. 1

We have a dear friend whom we have known for many years. She is a widow in her early forties, very attractive, with her own home and enough capital behind her to ensure that she need never work again.

She has always wanted to have her own fashion business. She certainly could start such a scheme. She has undoubted flair judging by the garments she has designed for herself over the years. She is highly intelligent, she could sell her product well and, of course, she has the capital to start her own business.

About every six months Jessica rings us up with some new angle she is working on towards her goal. She is always very excited and would like to see us immediately to discuss her next move. We talk through the idea — it is always a good one — offer advice and retire gracefully. Nothing happens for six months and then we repeat the exercise. It is our belief that Jessica will never get her business ideas off the ground, though undoubtedly we will have many happy hours talking about the possibilities for years to come. 'Ah,' you say, 'well that is not so surprising, she does not need to work. She has sufficient money to live on.' This is true, but we do not believe it to be the core of the problem. Her problem lies in the fact that she does not really have the commitment. Starting her own business is a nice thing to talk about, but she is 'playing at it'.

This is a symptom you must watch for very carefully in yourself. After all — we all have pipe dreams — things we would like to do, things we talk about doing but which we know we will never achieve. The idea of being one's own boss is a very attractive one. What you have to analyse is whether you have the commitment to make the dream a reality.

Case History No. 2

The stories are legion of men from humble beginnings creating vast empires with nothing to help them but a pound in their pocket and a dream. For every one famous name, however, there are thousands of men and women who have achieved their goal, albeit on a smaller scale.

We do some occasional consultancy work for a knitwear manufacturer. Despite the difficulties in today's textile trade, the company is enormously successful. Their founder, Ben, started work on a market stall nearly fifty years ago. It was hard work, very hard, but he attended the markets every day he could and found that his biggest sales were generated from knitwear. After about ten years he started his own manufacturing company. Today it supplies most of the major mail order companies and retail outlets in this country, while many much larger companies than his have gone bankrupt in the teeth of the recession.

Ask Ben to what he attributes his success and staying power, and he will show you his hands. Even today, when there is a nip in the air, they are covered in chilblains, the legacy of ten years work on market stalls. 'These old hands tell me,' he says, showing his poor red fingers, 'that business achievement is not easy. That you can never sit back on your laurels and say you've made it. They constantly remind me of what it was like on the market stall and ensure that I make certain I never go back there.' And how does he do that? By working hard to stay one step ahead of the game, never relaxing for a moment.

It is not easy but it has its compensations. Ben may have chilblains, but he has a brand new Jaguar every twelve months!

2. Family backing — are they going to be able to cope with it all?

'Annual income twenty pounds, annual expenditure nineteen pounds nineteen and sixpence, result happiness. Annual income twenty pounds, annual expenditure twenty pounds ought and six, result misery.' Charles Dickens.

Most of us from time to time have been faced with the need to reduce our standard of living. No one finds it easy and few of us really succeed unless faced with really dire difficulties. We believe it is unrealistic for you to seriously contemplate a dramatic change in your life style when you are trying to start a business. When you are working hard, when you are under pressure and probably more stress than normal, it is *not* the moment to disturb your creature comforts.

What applies to you equally well applies to your family. Even if your family are prepared in the beginning to make sacrifices to help you start your business, as months go by, it will become increasingly difficult for them not to resent the situation — particularly if there is no immediate tangible improvement. This, coupled with the inevitability of your being pre-occupied and over-worked, can lead to enormous conflict. These stresses are far more damaging to the growth of a business than any temporary cash flow difficulty.

Let us try and analyse the problems, one by one.

First, the financial implications. It is no good going into business in the hopes that ultimately the business will make a profit from which you can draw a salary. Unless you have unlimited personal capital resources, and few of us have, you must budget that from day one you should receive the right rate for the job. It may well be for the first few months you are unable to draw your salary, but in preparing any budget figures (*see* Chapter 9) you must allow for this salary, and at the first possible moment you must start drawing it. After all if you are not making money what on earth are you in business for anyway?

Assuming it will be a few months before you anticipate you can start drawing a healthy salary, you need to ensure that in the meantime you will be able to support yourself, and if you have one, your family. We cannot emphasise enough that stress is the real enemy to starting a business. You will have enough problems to consider without wondering how you are going to be able to pay the mortgage or feed the children.

First work out how much it will cost you to live without any dramatic cut-backs for the first four months. It may well be that you have a nest egg which will tide you over this period. It may be that you have a husband/wife who can keep the family finances afloat while you get established. Alternatively, of course, you may well be able to raise some money to live on from your friendly bank manager or building society. If, however, you have none of these advantages, there is a scheme available currently called the *Enterprise Allowance* which will make you a weekly grant while you establish your business. Details of this scheme are available through the Job Centre and at the moment such a scheme is only available if you have been unemployed for three months.

We must stress at this stage that if you have a family and no visible means of supporting them while you establish your business, in our view you would be extremely unwise to start. This, of course, is an appalling generalisation but without the benefit of being able to look at an individual case, in most instances we believe you would be stacking the odds too high against you.

On a personal level, it is imperative that you have moral support from your family. In a way, if you have no family commitments you are in the best possible position for starting your own business. Certainly coping with a young family and a new business is a potential recipe for disaster — all that noise and those sleepless nights! Having said that, a close family unit can provide tremendous security and stability in your darkest moments. Strong opposition and a lack of understanding from your partner, however, is to be avoided at all costs. Resigned acceptance is not enough.

In our view you have got to have not only complete backing from your partner, but full support and involvement in your project. If your family are not right behind you one hundred per cent – do not take the plunge. Their support is that important.

Case History No. 1

One of our main business interests centres round a company which designs and constructs exhibition stands. About four years ago the Managing Director approached us. He had recently been made redundant and wanted to start his own business in the exhibition industry, in which he was highly qualified. We decided to form a company which would provide the spring board for any business opportunities that came along. Having satisfied the various legal requirements by minuting the appointment of directors, shareholders, company secretary and registered office, our first job was to vote John (our colleague) a salary to keep him in a manner to which he felt he should be accustomed. On the face of it this was a pretty stupid thing to do when we had no business, no immediate prospects and therefore no visible means of income. In fact it was the right decision. With three small children and a mortgage, it was impossible for John to earn less than the amount we had voted him without serious depletion in his standard of living. Therefore any decision we made in the future as to the development of the company, had to be made in the light of having this fixed commitment to John. The company is doing very well, and though it has suffered from the odd ups and downs, John drew his salary from the very first month and has continued to do so ever since.

Case History No. 2

A little vignette from the life of Deborah Fowler! The first time I went into business I was in the throes of a divorce, with two children to bring up. My house was rented and I had no capital. The £450 overdraft which my bank manager kindly lent me to start the business, I mostly used for keeping the family fed! From this humble beginning I established a business. I acquired venture capital, new premises and partners and the business grew and grew. However years later, I still found I was operating on a shoestring — still trying to catch up with myself all the time. I am convinced that this symptom was a hangover from my early struggles. I went into business without properly planning for my family's future. The message, therefore, is that if you start by planning a survival campaign for your family, you will launch your business from a properly organised base, which gives it a far better chance of survival.

3. Product knowledge — are you sure you know what you are doing?

Ask any banker or financial institution about new businesses. They will quote you appalling statistics concerning the number of businesses that fail where the principals have had no previous knowledge of their trade. In our own case, one of us would like to be a builder, and the other a photographer (we leave you guessing as to which is which!). However, there is no possibility of either of us taking up the trade of our choice, since we are certain that we do not have knowledge to earn our living.

A sound product knowledge, we believe, is very important and we strongly advise you not to attempt to go into business in an area about which you know nothing. Having said that, of course, you can learn.

Product knowledge therefore really falls into two categories — you can exploit an existing skill or acquire a new one.

It may well be that you have worked in a sector of industry for some years and have seen that there is a gap in the market into which you can introduce a new type of product or service. Alternatively you may simply feel that the market is large enough for you to start a little company in the same field. It is obviously ideal if you can go into business with such a solid base of experience. You will have a good background knowledge of suppliers, pricing structures, staffing requirements, and probably above all, customers. In these circumstances however, you have to watch very carefully that because you have had such a good knowledge of the industry, you are not too complacent about starting your own business. You cannot compare the achievements of an existing business with what is likely to happen to you in the first few months of trading.

In contrast you may have had no previous experience in the trade of your choice. This situation applies to a surprising number of people. While struggling on and off a bus in a hot and dirty city, there can be few of us who have not wished that we were growing tomatoes in Devon, or some such thing. However, there is a lot more to growing tomatoes than meets the eye!

We would suggest, therefore, that if you have had no experience you should go out and get some before you start your own business. It does not have to be for a long time — a few months or even weeks may be sufficient for a non-technical trade. Time spent learning the ropes from someone who knows what they are doing can save you hours and hours of research, not to mention hideous mistakes when you come to do it for yourself. If, for example, your aspirations have an artistic bent — you have been making furniture for years as a hobby and you decide you are going to be a cabinet maker — in our view, you still need the experience of working in the trade. 'Why?', you say, 'I know the sort of furniture I want to make. All my friends love it. It has my own particular style. I do not want anybody to teach me how to do it differently.' That is not the point. If you work in a joinery for a few months, in as humble a capacity as you like, you will learn where they buy their timber and what sort of price they pay, where they obtain their tools, and a whole host of production short cuts that would have never occurred to you. Perhaps, most important of all, you will also learn what sort of price you can command for your furniture.

In conclusion; acquire as much knowledge as you possibly can about the product or service you intend to offer. The short cut to this is not original research, but picking the minds and experience of someone who is actually doing it. A little knowledge may be a dangerous thing but it is a lot less dangerous than no knowledge at all.

Case History No. 1

We have two friends called Mary and Jonathan. When they were married about ten years ago Jonathan, who was an accountant, had just bought an old farm in the Lake District. After years in the City he decided that he wanted to open a restaurant and bar, and Mary was only too happy to fall in with his plans. Shortly before their marriage, however, Mary got cold feet. Although they are a very likeable couple and make a very good mine host and hostess, they had absolutely no experience in the catering trade. Mary decided that she should remedy this and took a job in an hotel in Dorchester as a general 'dogsbody'. It meant living in and working a 60-hour week, for which she got paid the princely sum of £13. In addition, the hotel was run by a little Italian, whose principle aim in life was to pinch the bottoms of his female staff as often as possible!

As you can imagine, Jonathan was dead against it. It meant that almost immediately after their marriage they would have to be separated. But Mary insisted, and how right she was. She worked in Dorchester for four months and learnt everything she could about the catering trade. A year later they opened their restaurant and it was a huge success, but not without considerable teething troubles on the way. Today if you asked Jonathan to what he attributes the success of his restaurant he will put it down to Mary's experience.

Case History No. 2

Another well documented story of success I think proves our point. No doubt you will have heard of the retired American engineer who became upset by watching his daughter lugging a heavy pushchair up and down a flight of stairs, whilst she attempted to keep control of his newly acquired grandson under the other arm. The result of his anxiety — the world famous McClaren Baby Buggy — has revolutionised the lives of women with toddlers. Many a caring grandparent must have pondered on the problem before — it took an engineer to solve it.

4. Market research — are you sure anyone wants to know?

Marketing is the linchpin in every business.

Get it right and you can make a fortune. Get it wrong and however good the product or service you have to offer, you will have no business at all.

There are really two aspects to marketing. You have to provide a service or product that people want, and you have to provide it at the right price. These two requirements go hand in hand — your wonderful invention might well be capable of revolutionizing modern civilisation as we know it, but only if you offer it at the right price!

An important point to note here is that the 'right' price is not necessarily the cheapest price. In fact, very many businesses founder because they are selling their goods too cheaply. Not only are they not making the profits they should, but there is a strong tendency for a buyer to think that if an article is too cheap, it is no good.

Before you attempt to set up in business, you must undertake very thorough market research. Even if you think you know your trade well, it is still vital that you view the market from the position of a brand new business. The market reaction to an established business is completely different to that of an unknown name. Many ventures fail because the principal does not realise this.

You should undertake the market research yourself. There is no substitute for firsthand knowledge. Also — and here we will probably be linched for saying so — there is a tendency among advertising and marketing men to tell you what you *want* to hear. It is not a wilful attempt to deceive — it is just that in their profession it is necessary for them to be enthusiastic about absolutely everything!

Market research need not be terribly time consuming. Before you start pounding the pavements and collating a census, stop and think about your market. By approaching the right person so much work can be done for you.

Let us give you an example. Supposing you decided to start manufacturing children's clothes. Despite the recession, there are still a great many manufacturers in this country, and of course there is the constant threat of cheap imports. You must find a gap in the market. Your instant reaction might well be to interview 1,000 mums, from different social groupings, to seek their advice. Such a survey would take days and days, not to mention money in petrol and paperwork. You can short cut all that by going to see the children's buyers of one or two chain stores. They will tell you immediately what lines do not shift and what lines sell so well, there is always a stock shortage. Unlike 'Mrs. Bloggs', they state categorically, for instance, that red sells better than blue, that dungarees sell better than dresses, but not over six years old, and a host of such useful statistics. It is a buyer's job to anticipate trends, and if you ask the right questions he will be able to tell you what will be popular next year, which is far more relevant to you than what 'Mrs. Bloggs' is dressing little 'Jimmy' in this year.

We have cited one example, but what applies to the textile trade applies to every other. Do not approach the consumer, at any rate in a detailed way — go to somebody who is responsible for supplying him. Go, if necessary, to some of your future competitors. Make up an excuse for getting your foot in the door and talking to somebody who could help you. You have got to be cheeky. Goodness knows, you need to be that to go into business on your own anyway!

14

In summary: define very carefully your customer profile and how much he, or she, will be prepared to pay for what you have to offer. Get it right. Time spent at this stage is time well spent. It is no good realising you have made a mistake when your shelves are lined with the wrong type of stock.

Case History No. 1

A colleague of ours was involved, some years ago, in the marketing of a commercial product in graphic and drawing office supply, which today is a household name. You would never think so now, but ten years ago the company was in such trouble that they could not see their way to paying the following month's salaries. The management were at their wits end, they just could not see what was wrong. The product was a good one and had a wide appeal — from commercial art studios to schools. In desperation they called in a top marketing man. With only two or three weeks before the company would have to fold, he had to work quickly. He did. He doubled the selling price of every single item that the company produced. Two things happened. First, the business instantly became extremely profitable. Second — and this is the fascinating part — orders started rolling in at a considerably increased rate. The effect on cash flow was dramatic. Within a few weeks the company was saved.

Quite clearly they had been underselling their products. The only way the public could judge whether they were any good was by their price, and the price apparently had suggested that they were not. Since then, the company has learnt the lesson and continued to flourish.

Case History No. 2

Like everything, marketing is very susceptible to timing.

About ten years ago a friend of ours opened an off licence in a small Berkshire village. It was a time when people from all income groups were starting to travel abroad regularly and for the first time the British family was taking a real interest in wine. Our friend, Diana, who had recently moved to Berkshire from London, had noticed a slow but steady trend in London bistros to sell own label wine. She felt it was a good thing for two reasons. First, having the restaurant's name printed on the wine label was good publicity, but secondly it took the mystery out of wine buying. So there, in the heart of leafy Berkshire, 'Chateau Diana' was launched. In the early days, she simply bought two litre bottles of red and white wine from a branded importer, scraped off the label and substituted her own. She then sent a mailing list round all the local farmers, who she considered had plenty of money and liked their booze! Within a matter of weeks she had established an enormous reputation and people were coming from miles to buy her wine.

Bear in mind that ten years ago very few supermarkets had off licences, and certainly none of them were selling own label wine.

Diana had a marvellous run for two years and then sales began to dwindle. Trendy off licence chains were starting to offer own label wine and so were several supermarkets. Diana had had her day and luckily she knew it and pulled out of the business. She had made a lot of money though — *just by correctly assessing her market* — *at the right time*.

5. Selling — are you able to sell — your soul among other things?

We do not believe that a business can suceed without a good salesman.

You see, in the establishment of your business, it is not simply a question of being able to sell your product or service.

Practically every one needs some form of financial backing to his or her business. You have to be able to convince a backer that you are worth backing — that means you have to be able to 'sell' the idea to him. With the high proportion of companies going into liquidation in recent years, suppliers are very loath to give automatic credit. You will have to 'sell' your stability and reliability to your major suppliers in order to obtain credit — so vital to the early days of cash flow. You may well need premises. Landlords are very cautious about renting premises to new businesses. You are going to have to 'sell' the viability of your idea to your landlord in order to get a lease. If you are selling consumer goods or services you will most likely benefit from press coverage. You have to be able to 'sell' your business ideas to newspaper reporters.

We could go on and on like this. Every step you take in the development of your business is easier, far easier, if you have the ability to put across your idea.

Over the years and especially in the compilation of this book, we have talked to a great many bank managers. One in particular is a very old friend of ours, who believes in bending over backwards to help establish a new business. We asked him what was the secret formula — what made him agree to a proposal. What he said was most revealing. Nine times out of ten he turns down potential customers, not because of the content of their proposal, but because of their inability to convince him that they know what they are talking about. They simply do not have the ability to sell themselves.

A firm belief in your own business very often turns you into a first class salesman. The business is 'your baby'. If you truly believe in what you are doing, you are its best ambassador. But here it is terribly important for you to be self-critical. You might be producing a wonderful product, at the right price, and it could be something for which the market place is screaming. But even in those ideal circumstances, the business could fail through your inability to get across to your market the extent of your achievement.

Sales are the life blood of your business. Without sales you have no business. So what do you do if in your heart of hearts you know you cannot sell? You join forces with someone who can. You can take on a partner, a salesman or an agent. You can operate through a wholesaler or industrial distributor. It depends so much on the nature of your business. In Chapter 13 we explore these various options in detail.

Suffice to say here, choose with care the person who is to be responsible for your selling. Salesmen are best at selling themselves. You need to get behind all the jargon and establish in your own mind that he or she has got the necessary 'grit in the guts' to work hard as well as talk hard.

The message for this chapter is: you need a good product, a good market, sufficient capital and a well organised administration, but 'sales maketh the business'.

Case History No. 1

A little philosophizing from Alan Fowler:
　　'I trained as an accountant, though I fondly imagine that I do not

think like one! Over the years I have helped many many people establish their businesses, turned losses into profits, and sometimes, sadly, helped people clear up the mess after a failure. I do, however, know my limitations. I could not sell a life belt to a drowning man. I watch with admiration as my partners close a deal, but I could not begin to do it myself.

For this reason I have never gone into business on my own. I always try to get together with a partner, who is a salesman. It is interesting to reflect that on the one or two occasions where my partner has not been a salesman, the business has not taken off. I have learnt my lesson. It is my golden rule. Even if I discovered the secret of eternal youth, I would get someone else to sell it.'

Case History No. 2

We have a friend who is a leading chemist in the cosmetics industry. For years he has worked for the top cosmetic houses and is well known and respected in the trade. His background training and qualifications are impeccable and he has a worldwide reputation.

A few years ago he decided he had had enough working for big companies and set up his own small laboratory. The idea was that he should offer a freelance service, developing and producing particular formulae for beauty products and cosmetics for any cosmetic house that required them.

He asked our advice at the time and we thought it was a wonderful idea. The fact remains that his little business has never really got off the ground. Why? He has tremendous experience, is highly qualified and can produce some wonderful products . . . *but he cannot sell*.

6. The wrong motive — are you desperate and can you still be rational?

Need is not enough but it can be the spur.

Inevitably, some of you who read this book will have been made redundant, have been retired early, or perhaps have never even had a job. In these circumstances you may feel desperate. Desperate for two reasons — frankly because you need the money, but perhaps also because you feel unfulfilled, inadequate and unable to cope with the hours of leisure. As we all know, unemployment can be soul destroying.

If you are in this situation your suffering could well be increased by the knowledge that you are unlikely to ever find another job. Either your trade is on the decline, or you are the wrong age, or perhaps you live in a depressed area where unemployment is rife.

So the only answer is, if nobody is going to help you, you should help yourself. If this book helps one person in those circumstances to get a successful business off the ground, then it will have been worthwhile. 'Having a go' has to be better than sitting around with no hope and no future.

Having said that, please, please be careful. We hope the preceding chapters will have helped you to decide whether you are in the right frame of mind, and in the right circumstances, to take the step. If your response to the questions posed in our chapter headings is in general 'NO', then however desperate you are, do not go ahead. Business is all about risks and commitment. You could easily make your position so much worse.

Your thought process must not be — 'I have some redundancy money, what sort of business shall I start?' It needs to be 'I have always thought if I had the money I would be a . . ., so now I can fulfil my ambitions.' In other words the basic idea needs to be with you before you are made redundant.

Similarly, do not start a business in a half-hearted way — thinking that you will do it until a job turns up. If you approach a venture with this attitude, we can guarantee the business will fail. You must take up the challenge whole-heartedly, give it everything you have got. Make the decision and stick to it or you will simply fall at the first fence — and what is the point of being wiser after the event?

Enough of the gloom. Redundancy or early retirement can give you the opportunity to start the business you have always wanted. The need to succeed can lead you into a way of life which will be both fulfilling and rewarding. It can take you places that cushioned employment could never have done; you will discover hidden resources you did not know you possessed and you will gain confidence and stature.

So, however difficult your current circumstances may be, if you think you have got what it takes, stick with us.

Case History No. 1

We have a good friend called Harry who has had many years experience in the mail order business. A few months ago he had a 'punch-up' with his boss and left his latest employment. For years he had watched mail order companies make mistakes and he reckoned, with all his experience he could do a better job.

He had virtually no capital of his own, though with a good idea, that should not matter. Within a month he had his own small catalogue, which he mailed initially to a thousand people. Within three weeks he was out of the mail order business because the mailing had not worked and he had not had enough orders to justify his outlay.

Harry rushed into this position for just one reason — or perhaps we should say, three — a wife, a mortgage and a brand new baby. He had to get income and he had to get income quickly. The moment the business did not come across with the necessary cash, he gave it up — barely three weeks after he had started it.

And the result of all this? He is £1,000 out of pocket. Not a big sum, some might say, but it is a lot of money when you are unemployed.

Don't be like Harry. Think first, act second. And when you do act, stick with it, however hard it is.

Case History No. 2

Here is an example of an ideal way to start a business.

In the course of one of our activities we are involved in providing fashion photography. One of the models we use is a man in his later thirties called John. You would all recognise his face. For over fifteen years he has appeared in many mail order catalogues, T.V. commercials, newspaper and magazine advertisements. His looks have stood the test of time very well — lucky chap! However, a model's career cannot last for ever and when he married, about eight years ago, he started a small business with his wife, restoring antique furniture. He has built the business slowly — he has really had no choice with modelling assignments often taking him abroad. However, gradually, year by year, he is establishing a reputation, both with the trade and with the public and he is making a steady profit.

If John never received another modelling job, he has a business which will now support him, his wife and two small children. John knew he could not be employed until sixty-five and he did something about it.

If redundancy is inevitable for you, do not put your head in the sand and wait for it to happen. Do something — *act now*.

'The Decision'

SHALL I START MY OWN BUSINESS?

[Tick here]

<table>
<tr><td style="border:1px solid;width:120px;height:100px;"></td><td style="width:60px;"></td><td style="border:1px solid;width:120px;height:100px;"></td></tr>
<tr><td align="center">YES</td><td></td><td align="center">NO</td></tr>
</table>

We wish we could make it easy for you. It would be wonderful to be able to summarise the preceding six chapters in one telling phrase which would give you your 'YES' or 'NO'.

We can best help by summarising for you a check list of DO'S and DON'TS, as follows:

DON'T start your own business:
1. If you cannot work hard — through lack of inclination or ill health.
2. If you do not possess complete confidence in your product or service.
3. If you do not have family backing.
4. If you do not know enough about your chosen trade and are not prepared to learn.
5. If no one is interested in what you have to offer.
6. If you cannot sell, nor find anyone to help you.
7. If desperation is forcing you into it.

DO start your own business:
1. If, not only are you not afraid of hard work, but you can also cope with stress.
2. If you feel positively vocational about your venture.
3. If you have no family commitments, or, alternatively, the full backing of your family.
4. If you have learnt your trade.
5. If there is that all important gap in the market — just waiting for you.
6. If you can sell — or join forces with someone else who can.
7. If you are not letting desperation be your master.
8. IF YOU HAVE THE DEDICATION AND COMMIT-MENT TO SUCCEED — HOWEVER LONG THE STRUGGLE — HOWEVER HARD THE BATTLE.

The answer is NO? Put this book away and read it again in six months time. People change, circumstances change. You may well start your own business one day, but you are sensible enough to realise that now is not the right time.

The answer is YES? Well done. It is going to be tough-going, but read on . . . together we will get through it!

'GETTING IT TOGETHER'

This section of the book deals with the establishment of your business.

It is terribly important, however modest your initial business aspirations, that you start trading from the right base. In the early days, your impatience to get started can lead you to make a number of snap decisions which, as the business develops, you will regret. It is easy, for example, to accept finance from the first person who offers it, to go into partnership with that nice chap over the road because you like him, not because you recognize his abilities.

What you have to consider in the setting up of your business is that the decisions you make now most probably will be affecting you in fifteen or twenty years time. It is difficult, but what you need to define, right from the beginning, is your ultimate goal. The decisions you take on the formation of the business should be heavily influenced by what you ultimately want to achieve.

The establishment of a business is not just a question of a few formalities. How well you tackle the problem can greatly influence the future prosperity of your venture. Take time, take trouble, take care — it is worth doing properly.

7. The other, other half

Starting your own business is one long decision! Having decided on the nature of your trade or service, the very next decision that you need to take is whether you are going to embark on your business alone . . . or with someone else. It is important that you make your mind up on this aspect before any other, since the acquisiton of a partner could greatly alter the way in which you form your business.

In Chapter 8 we detail the ways in which you can set up a partnership — the legal obligations and options open to you. In this chapter we are primarily concerned with relationships — indeed establishing whether you need, or would benefit from, a partner or partners.

Every business can be divided into three main areas of operation:

Production

Sales

Administration

It is vital that your business has at its disposal someone who can understand and handle these three basic ingredients. We know several people who have 'gone it alone' — with two of the skills mentioned above and a quick crash course in the third! We think it fair to say however that most people come unstuck in at least one of these areas.

Even if you can handle all aspects of running your business, there are three other main reasons why you might take a partner:

Money

Premises

Moral support

Money is probably the main reason businessmen go into partnership — one of them has the idea, the other the finance, so they get together.

The importance of premises of course, varies enormously from trade to trade. To cite an extreme example, one could not possibly contemplate starting a riding stable from a first floor flat. Put your 'horsey' skills together with a farmer who has a few old barns and suddenly you have a partnership!

The third cause — moral support, may seem like the poor relation compared with the others, but it is probably the most important. Most of us need companionship, advice, comfort, someone with whom to celebrate triumphs, someone with whom to commiserate over disasters.

Business partnership sounds rather like marriage doesn't it. It is really — certainly it can be wonderful if it goes right and terrible if it goes wrong!

What you have to decide is whether you have the necessary accomplishments not to need a partner. Having decided that, you need to consider whether you are in the right circumstances not to need a partner. If you are, then away you go. Certainly there are many advantages in trading alone. You really are your own boss, in every sense of the word. You can take your business decisions without reference to anyone — except perhaps your bank manager! You can build the business at a pace to suit yourself, develop it in any direction you like. Just do not let all that power go to your head. However successful you become, never lose the ability to take advice. That is the way to stay successful.

Let us now consider the question of going into business with someone else.

Golden Rule No. 1

First, there is absolutely no point in going into business with someone whose skills are the same, or similar, to your own. The whole point of joining forces with someone is that you can combine your complementary abilities to form a stronger base from which to launch your venture. In addition, apart from the business benefiting from as many varied skills as possible, you are much less likely to have relationship difficulties with a partner whose responsibilities within the business are different from yours.

Golden Rule No. 2

As a general rule we do not favour going into business with friends. The ideal relationship is that where two people get together to form a business because commercially it makes sense for them so to do. Having established that business, if the partnership is successful, a friendship will grow. The problem with mixing friends and business is that so often one begins the business partnership on the wrong basis. In drawing up the basis for a partnership agreement, friends tend to be much too nice to each other! In any partnership agreement you want the best possible deal — you must negotiate for what you want out of the business and make sure you get it. It is far more difficult to be ruthless with dear old Fred, who you meet for a pint once a week. The awful part is that if you establish your business relationship on the wrong footing, you end up by resenting dear old Fred — you lose a partnership, probably a business, and certainly a friend. It is difficult to generalise, but never, never go into partnership with someone because he or she is a friend — if you must do it, make sure your friend is someone with whom you can be utterly frank. Make sure they realise you are in business for money . . . not love!

Golden Rule No. 3

In forming any sort of business partnership, it is terribly important that you try and relate skill and effort to financial reward. The 'sleeping partner' is the prime example of a relationship fraught with hazard. You want to start a business. You have a good idea, but no money. That is a standard situation in which most of us find ourselves. You find someone with money. He puts up, say, £10,000 and you go into business. You form a company, split it fifty/fifty and away you go. When ten years later your business is turning over two million pounds a year, due to your hard work, enterprise and skill, how do you feel about the man who once lent you £10,000 and now receives 50% of everything you earn? We guarantee you will hate his guts. You will have forgotten that without him you would never have had a business. You just know that while you worked and worked, he simply sat back and took the money. It will never even occur to you to wonder how hard he had to work to earn that £10,000 he lent you, or to wonder at the faith he had in you when you were nobody. You are probably saying that you would be different — at this very moment you are no doubt full of self righteous indignation. You are wrong, we have seen it happen over and over again.

It is not an easy situation, we realise that. If you find someone interested enough to join you in a partnership — whether it is a financial one or not, you are so pleased that they are prepared to be involved in your venture you naturally want to offer them an attractive proposition. Do, however, try and look to the future. If you are going to do all or most of the work in the long term, your partnership agreement should reflect this. If on the other hand you are a mad professor, who has developed some wonderful invention, which somebody else is going to produce and sell, it is not unreasonable, in the long term, that they make most of the profits.

It is terribly difficult to advise you how to avoid pitfalls in general terms. Every partnership agreement is an individual affair and it is not easy to generalise. However, as a guide, start with the basics. If your partner is putting up the money and you are mainly doing the work, then two clauses need to be written into your agreement. Your partner needs to receive interest on his loan, which should be expressed as an agreed rate above bank base rate, and you should receive a salary which is appropriate for the job you are doing. Thus, so far as the foundation of the relationship is concerned, honour is satisfied.

You should, however, bear in mind that as your business grows your job will grow in stature — added responsibilities should mean a greater salary. Therefore in your salary clause you should stipulate that your remuneration will be reviewed from time to time and that in the case of any dispute with your partner, an agreed person, such as your solicitor or accountant, should act as arbitrator. Having established this agreement, you are both being paid for what you put into the venture, now and in the future. On this basis, there should be no dispute about splitting the profits on the originally agreed basis. In other words, go back to our example of the man who built his business into a two million pound company after ten years, but still splits the profits fifty/fifty with his original partner. If this man is the principal of a business turning over two million pounds, then he is justified in drawing a salary of, say, £30,000 or £40,000 per year. In such a situation it suddenly becomes a great deal less onerous having to share the balance of the profits with his partner.

In Chapter 8 we look at the legalities of a partnership — here we ask you to consider its morality. Take your expectations for the first five years of trading (it can only be an educated guess). Then form your partnership in such a way as to give back financial reward in roughly the same proportion as the skill, hard work and financial help which is to be poured into the business over that period.

Golden Rule No. 4

Like your partner. You would not marry someone you did not like, would you? No, we are not leading you round in circles. On the one hand we did say we think it advisable that your business partner should not be a friend first. On the other hand, we all have instinctive reactions to people. If the vibes are wrong do not go ahead. It is a sobering thought, but in many instances it is quite possible that you will spend more time with your business partner than you will with your marriage partner. It is too big a chunk out of your life to spend with someone you do not like.

Golden Rule No. 5

Finally, and this is a difficult one, when you draw up that partnership agreement or form a joint company, do sit down and build in a formula for breaking up. Agree terms now, while the relationship is amicable, which you both consider to be fair, so that if things do go wrong, you both have your 'out'. This is terribly important and do check the wording with your solicitor.

Case History No. 1

It's us! We met five years ago. A lawyer friend of ours introduced us because I (Deborah) had told him I needed a little financial guidance — no money, just guidance. Alan thoroughly examined my company's books. I did need financial help and money — quite a lot! Alan provided both. He joined the board of my company (that required a great deal of soul searching on my part, as I had previously always operated alone) and we worked together for two years before, as they say, our friendship blossomed.

Married now, with several joint business interests, we really enjoy working together. We do, however, have two completely separate relationships. We would never use our personal relationship to score a point in a business sense, because . . . the business relationship came first.

Case History No. 2

About ten years ago, when I (Alan) was living in Buckinghamshire, I was asked to advise two women who wished to start a dress shop in Beaconsfield. On the face of it they seemed an ideal combination. Elizabeth had flair, good dress sense and natural poise. Her home and her clothes reflected tremendous ability with colour combinations. An articulate, intelligent woman, she could put across her ideas well. Her proposed partner, Barbara, was frankly a bit of a rough diamond! Her background was trading from market stalls. She had an eye for a bargain and she could haggle like a 'good 'un'! Profit in my view is very much a state of mind, and Barbara had that kind of mind. She knew that the success of their business lay in the difference between what she could buy goods for and what she could sell them for. Colour, style, taste, quality, were all very well in their place, but what Barbara wanted to do was make money.

Their partnership was an unmitigated disaster. Yes they had complementary skills, but they were too different. As people they had absolutely nothing in common. They could not agree about anything, and believe me, as piggy in the middle, it was hell on earth!

During the first few months of trading their business made a substantial profit, and when the inevitable breakup came (Barbara left and Elizabeth stayed — she had money as well as flair!), I thought we could look forward to more tranquil days. Not so, within a further six months the business had failed. Why? Basically because it no longer had Barbara — 'the wheeler-dealer'. The message here is that complementary skills must not be so diverse that you and your colleague have nothing in common. It is back to Golden Rule No. 4. If you are looking for the other, other half you must strive for the best of all possible worlds. You and your partner must be different . . . but the same.

8.   'The Set Up'

Of course you can change the structure of your business as it develops —
many people do so in response to rapid development. However it is
better to take a long term view of your likely needs and requirements and

plan your trading methods accordingly. You are very brave to be contemplating going into business with so many odds stacked against success — you must shorten them any way you can and laying down the right foundations is terribly important. The first golden rule is that business affairs must be kept completely separate from your personal dealings. You must maintain proper accounting records and have a separate bank account. This rule is fundamental to every business, and with this firmly in mind let us look at the three *main* ways of trading.

1. *The sole trader*

The moment you have finished reading this book you can dash away, start trading and you are in business! This is the simplest and therefore most common form of business entity since there are so few legal requirements involved. People are inclined to think that sole trading is restricting, that this sort of business is most suited to 'one man and his boy'. This is not the case and there are a number of very large concerns in this country operating on such a basis. As a sole trader, you can employ as many people as you like and operate as big a business as you like, and in a general trading sense the only legal requirements are as follows:

(a) Keeping an up-to-date set of books and records for tax purposes. The tax authorities have the right to inspect these and will do so from time to time.

(b) If your sales go over a certain limit you will have to register for VAT. Indeed in some cases it is of benefit to register even if your immediate turnover is likely to be below the limit. It is important to contact your local VAT office as soon as you start trading to establish what rules apply to your business.

(c) If you decide to employ anyone you will have to comply with a wide range of legislation and will be required to make PAYE returns — *see* Chapter 12 for full details.

The advantages of being a sole trader are obvious. One of the many reasons you may be attracted to starting your own business is that you want to be your own boss. The sole trader is very much his own man. Apart from the normal tax returns, a requirement of any business, he has no shareholders or co-directors to whom he is answerable. His affairs are his own. Unlike a limited company there is no requirement to register his accounts for all the world to see. In a nation somewhat beleaguered by red tape, the sole trader will attract the very minimum — no small consideration!

The disadvantages however cannot be ignored. As a sole trader you will enjoy 100% of the profits from your business. You are also 100% responsible for its debts, unlike a limited partnership or company. Unsatisfied creditors can pursue you not only for the assets of the business, but also for your personal assets as well. For this reason, before embarking on business as a sole trader it might well be sensible to transfer your major assets, such as your house, into your wife/husband's name, so that in the event of failure at least your home is protected. This piece of advice is not intended to encourage you to have a cavalier attitude towards your debts, but particularly where children are involved, any business venture you undertake, in our view, should not, if at all possible, jeopardise the family home.

The other main disadvantage of the sole trader is that on the whole you will find it more difficult to raise capital. When an investor backs a sole trader he is backing a man rather more than a business, the inference being that if something happens to the man there is no business left. Of course many small companies are as dependent on their founder/director as a sole trader's business, but our experience would indicate that for commercial purposes, banks prefer to lend money to a formally structured company rather than to an individual trader. This attitude will also tend to apply with non-banking institutions and organisations from whom grants, capital or loan money may be sought.

2. *Partnerships*

Let's face it, successful marriages are not easy to come by these days and we think they are a great deal easier to achieve than a successful business partnership! We have dealt at length in the previous chapter about selecting the right partner so let us assume here that you are intending to go into business with the ideal partner for you.

The simplest form of partnership is merely an extension of the sole trader. Instead of one of you reaping the profits and carrying responsibility for the debts, two or more persons are involved. There is no legal requirement for a written partnership agreement, but it would be extremely foolish not to have such a document. Any solicitor can help you draw up a standard partnership agreement but we think it very important that you approach such an agreement with the right attitude of mind. It is impossible here to list all the clauses that might be required for every type of business. It is important however to accept that the time you are most likely to require reference to your written agreement is when the business is going wrong. You and your partner need to say to each other — 'what happens if the business is in terrible debt, if one of us is chronically ill, the premises have just burnt down and we hate each other's guts?' You must consider every eventuality — if one of you dies; if the business changes direction as it develops making the workload unequal; if one of you wishes to take your son or daughter into the business; if your views vary as to the business's development — one of you may be cautious, the other very ambitious. It goes on and on — it is an absolute minefield of potential conflict. We have talked to a number of experts on how best to resolve partnership disputes, for however good your written agreement you simply cannot cover every possible eventuality. One suggestion we had, which we think is a very good one, is to appoint a third party such as a trusted lawyer or accountant whose ruling you agree to accept in the event of a problem arising which you cannot resolve between you.

Most partnerships operate on a fifty-fifty basis but profits may be shared in agreed proportions according to the amount of work and expertise each partner will be applying to the business, and the amount of money they have each invested.

You can create a limited partnership. In this event one or more of the partners can opt for limited liability. This means that in the event of things going wrong the partners with limited liability are only liable to meet creditors claims up to the amount they have invested in the partnership. In other words, if the business failed with your firm owing Mr. Brown £10,000 but your limited liability was for say £2,000 it would be up to your partner to find the rest. It should be understood that in every partnership there must be one partner prepared to accept unlimited liability, and limited partners may not take part in the management of the business for obvious reasons. In the case of limited partnerships, these must be registered with the Registrar of Companies and there is a small stamp duty to pay on the formation of the partnership.

The advantages of a partnership are the same as that of the sole trader — it is cheap and easy to form and attracts the minimum of legislation. The disadvantages too are the same as with the sole trader, but there is one additional problem which cannot be ignored. With a partnership you are terribly dependent on your relationship with another person or persons. People change, circumstances change and particularly when things are difficult, the best relationships can go sour. Remember you are responsible for each other's actions. Whilst the bank account can be controlled by you and your partner having joint signatories on the cheques, there is nothing to stop one partner ordering, let us say, £25,000 worth of goods on behalf of the partnership, failure to pay for which would be your joint responsibility.

3. *The Limited Company*

A completely separate legal entity is created by the formation of a limited company. Company law is very complicated but the setting up of a small private company can be quickly and simply done for a comparatively small cost. You can approach the Registrar of Companies yourself, fill out the necessary forms and form a company without any legal advice. However we would strongly recommend that you employ the services of a solicitor to ensure that the company is properly set up. He will probably recommend that you buy an established company 'off the shelf'. To form a company you need a minimum of two directors, one of whom will also need to be company secretary, unless as in many cases, your solicitor volunteers for the appointment. There are considerable advantages in your solicitor acting as company secretary as there can be a degree of paperwork associated with the job — such as the drawing up of Minutes and filing of annual returns. However it should be remembered that he is not going to do it for love!

One of the early problems you will experience with the formation of a limited company is its name. If you buy a company 'off the shelf' it will have been given a name by the registration agent. The names they allocate to companies 'on the shelf' are all extremely odd! It is very unlikely that you will want to use the given name, in which case you might find a name which is acceptable to the Registrar of Companies. This legislation varies from that of the sole trader or partnership where you are perfectly entitled to call yourself 'Joe Bloggs Enterprises' regardless of how many businesses there are of the same name.

Although your solicitor will handle the establishment of a company for you there are various terms which we feel are worth briefly describing as follows:

Memorandum of Association
This is the basic document required to form a company and will need to be signed by two directors/shareholders. It states the company's name, the situation of the registered office and share capital. It also defines the objects of the company — the type of business in which it will be engaged. It is important that this description accurately covers your type of business.

Articles of Association
This document too is required for the formation of the company and deals with the internal regulations of the company and also requires the directors'/shareholders' signatures. Most Articles of Association are those set out in Table A of the Companies Act and only occasionally will they need modification.

Share Capital

Share Capital is the money a company obtains by issuing shares to its members. The capital of a company is described as follows:

(i) *Authorised Capital* — This is the nominal value of the shares which the company is authorised to issue at the time of its formation. The amount of capital involved will be partly determined by the amount of money the shareholders have to invest and partly by the likely future needs of the company. The authorised capital can be increased from time to time, as necessary.

(ii) *The Issued Capital* — This is the name given to that part of the authorised capital which has actually been issued to members.

(iii) *Paid Up Capital* — This is the name given to the amount of issued capital which has actually been paid for.

(iv) *The Uncalled Capital* — This is the name given to the authorised capital which has not yet been issued.

It should be noted that in the event of the company going into liquidation shareholders and directors will probably lose their paid up capital and will be required to provide the money for any issued capital for which they have not paid. This however is the full extent of their liabilities, unless they have entered into any personal guarantees on behalf of the company, or have traded in any way illegally.

Obviously the main advantage of forming a limited company is that your liability in the event of things going wrong will be limited to the amount of share capital you have invested in the business. Your home and all your personal assets will be safe.

The limited company also provides a structured framework within which you and your business partners can work. Unlike the partnership, there is less likelihood of confusion and disputes. Another advantage is that the limited company imposes a degree of discipline upon its directors. For example, annual accounts have to be prepared and filed with the Registrar of Companies. This means that every year you must employ a firm of accountants to prepare these figures. Their job is not purely to audit accounts for the Registrar of Companies — they should also give you their views and advice on the previous year's trading and how they see the future development of your company. Accountants vary enormously, of course, and just like every other species within the human race, they have their fair share of idiots! However, as a general rule a qualified outsider's view of your business should be of enormous benefit. As mentioned under the heading 'Sole Trader', generally financial institutions prefer to lend money to companies rather than individuals and certainly when it comes to borrowing substantial sums of money we would advise you to operate within a company structure.

Lastly, and by no means least, once you are regularly earning substantial sums of money, these are definite tax advantages in operating your business as a limited company.

Possibly the biggest disadvantage in forming a company is cost. Quite apart from the initial costs of setting up the company, in order to comply with the requirements of Company Law, there is the need for a continuing involvement with solicitors and accountants, which tends to be expensive! The annual audit fee is a case in point. Once you have formed a limited company you are committed to this, year in, year out. Companies are also subject to many more rules and regulations — you cannot escape the red tape in the way you can as a sole trader.

Using any of the three vehicles above, there are two ways of setting up a business without having to start from scratch.

Buying an existing business

The scale of such a transaction can, of course, vary enormously. It could be that you commit yourself to a substantial investment, involving the purchase of property and equipment, and perhaps taking on an obligation to existing staff. Alternatively, it may be just a question of buying what you consider to be a valuable name, plus the goodwill attached to it.

However, regardless of the size of the investment, we do strongly advise you to ask your accountant to carry out a thorough assessment as to the worth of the business before you commit yourself to the purchase. Very often a business, or part of a business, becomes available for purchase because it has hit financial difficulties. In these circumstances, before getting too excited about the possibility of picking up something for next to nothing, you need to think very carefully why the business is in financial trouble in the first place. You could simply be buying your way into a whole heap of trouble.

Over the years, I (Alan) have been involved in many, many acquisitions. Assessing the value of a business is difficult and although your solicitor and accountant should be able to help you, if the professional firm is a small one, they may not have had a great deal of experience in handling this type of transaction. I have listed below a few points to look out for, when you are considering the purchase of a business. They may seem obvious and your accountant or solicitor should investigate them without the need for prompting. However, you would be amazed how often really big issues are overlooked when it comes to business acquisition.

Assets

    (a) Freehold property — As well as establishing the value of any freehold, it is also important to check out planning use and whether the property conforms to the Health and Safety laws with regard to the number of people you wish to employ on the premises. You need to check that the premises are not subject to any mortgages and that there are no local development plans, such as road widening schemes, which would affect the property specifically. Also you should be aware of any larger scale planning proposals, such as motorway extensions, which might have an adverse impact on the locality.

    (b) Leasehold property — The same comments apply to a leasehold as with a freehold, with the addition that you want to check out very carefully the rent review position, and whether there are any onerous clauses in the lease, which might restrict your use of the premises.

    (c) Stock — Obviously, before purchasing any stock you have to assess its value, but the other point to consider is whether you really want it. The business may be up for sale because it has financial troubles, one of the reasons for which could be too much stock! Even if the stock is being sold off below its market value, do not just buy it because it looks a good bargain. Nine times out of ten, if the stock cannot fetch its true market value, there is something wrong with it.

    (d) Debtors — Very often in the acquisition of a company you will inherit the trade debts. Before you allow that debtor figure to be taken into account in assessing the purchase price of the business, you need to make sure that the debtors are good for their money. How old are the debts, how reliable are the debtors, what is their track record of payment? Adequate provision must be made for any doubtful debts.

    (e) Vehicles — Before taking on any vehicles check out the HP position. It sounds very obvious doesn't it, but you would be surprised how many people get caught by this one!

    (f) Patents/Trademarks/Trading Names — You might consider a particular patent, trademark or trading name to be one of the most valuable assets of your proposed purchase. These assets are not worth a jot though if they are not registered. Do check this out very carefully and insist that they are registered before any acquisition is made.

Liabilities

    (a) Trade Creditors — This is an area where you want to be

particularly careful before agreeing to take on the liability. Are the creditors really fully disclosed and will you have sufficient funds to settle creditors as they fall due?

(b) *Tax Liabilities* — The same general comments apply as with creditors. Make sure that your accountant has identified any contingent tax liabilities.

(c) *Pension Commitments* — If you are taking over a company with a pension scheme, check it out very carefully, since with even a small staff it can represent a big financial commitment.

(d) *Redundancy* — Inevitably, if you are going to take over a business, you are going to run it your way and your way will be different from the old regime. This will lead to staff changes and you need to establish in broad outline your redundancy liabilities if many changes are to be made.

(e) *Contracts of Employment* — You should check these out for any staff you intend to take on. You may find there are some onerous clauses with regard to length of notice, salary reviews and so forth.

(f) *Litigation* — You need to satisfy yourself that the business is not involved in any legal actions.

Warranties

You must obtain from the vendor a warranty that the assets and liabilities are what he says they are. Should you later uncover, say, a further £10,000 worth of creditors you must be able to pursue the vendor for that money. However, an important point to note here is whether he is good for the money. A warranty can be a singularly useless piece of paper if there is no cash to back it up! If you suspect that this is the case it should be reflected in the purchase price, or part of the purchase price should be withheld for an agreed period against the warranty commitment.

The Franchise Operation

This can be quite a good way for the first-time businessman to start his own venture, but you do have to be very careful indeed.

A number of very famous names in the high street, in areas such as catering and beauty products, have built their businesses by offering franchises. Dealing with a reputable company can prove very rewarding. It is impossible here to list every permutation there can be to a franchise relationship. However, the basic concept behind a franchise is that you are granted a licence to trade under the name of a well-established company. You may, for the sake of example, decide to take a franchise and open a restaurant in Birmingham trading as 'Jo's Hamburgers'. There are many ways of setting up the deal. It may be that you buy your property from 'Jo's Hamburgers', that you find your own property, or that you simply lease the restaurant from the company. You may have to equip the restaurant yourself to 'Jo's Hamburgers' specifications, or you may have the equipment provided for you. In any event, either you will have to make a lump sum payment or a continuing royalty payment — or both. In return, 'Jo's Hamburgers' provide you with their name, group marketing and advertising, advice and management supervision. Usually they will help you train your staff, and have group buying arrangements, which are far more advantageous than if you traded alone. With a good franchisor the list of services can be endless. However, possibly the single biggest advantage is that in joining a reputable franchise operation, your business venture is following a formula that works. In other words, if 'Jo's Hamburgers' are trading successfully in London, Manchester, Cardiff, and Edinburgh, there is every reason to suppose that your business will work in Birmingham.

The disadvantages are obvious. You are not your own boss in quite the same way as you would be 'going it alone', and of course, more important, you are likely to be committed to paying some form of royalty to the franchisor from your profits. However, that seems a small price to pay for assured business success.

Do take care though. Never undertake any form of franchise agreement without reference to your accountant or solicitor. You need to establish not only the legal implications of the franchise, but also its worth — should you really be spending £15,000 or whatever? Remember, there are some dishonest dealers in the franchise trade. Moreover, a number of companies have tried to set up franchise operations when they find themselves in serious financial trouble. It is a last ditch attempt on their part to save their company. As you will appreciate, selling several franchises at say £15,000 or £20,000 each can suddenly bring a great deal of much needed money into a company but it may not be enough to save it from bankruptcy. So seek professional advice before signing anything, and ask your solicitor to do a company search to find out as much as he can about your proposed franchisor. It does not matter how well known a name it might be — thoroughly check them out. Remember after the collapse of Rolls Royce, nothing is sacred!

We have outlined for you the three main ways of trading but quite clearly it is now time for us to come off the fence and give you our advice, which after all is what this book is all about. The first question you need to ask yourself is whether you are providing a service or a commodity. If the answer is a service, in other words you are selling your time, whether as a window cleaner, a typist or a consultant, then we would recommend that you operate as a sole trader or partnership. If on the other hand, you are selling a commodity — you are buying a raw material, or finished goods, putting them through some form of manufacturing or marketing process and then selling them on, as a general rule we think you should form a limited company.

Let us explain this in more detail. Where a service is concerned you are unlikely to attract enormous liabilities. If you are hiring out your expertise you may well need premises and some equipment but on a day-to-day operating basis you are not having to regularly invest sums of money in order to trade. Therefore if your business goes wrong you are unlikely to have amassed large debts.

So far as selling a commodity is concerned, in order to decide whether you need to form a limited company, we would ask you to look carefully at the ratio of costs between your time and the raw materials involved. For example, if you are a cabinet maker you will have to invest a comparatively small amount of money in buying the necessary wood but you will expend many hours turning that wood into furniture. In other words, your cash investment is small in relation to your eventual income. If however your business is importing leather goods from the Far East, presenting them in nice packages and selling them on to retail outlets in this country, your investment will be huge and your profit margin probably very small. You would only have to find that you had bought 10,000 leather purses but could only sell 9,100 and bang would go your profit! In other words if there is very little margin for error in your trading you are in the high risk business. In these circumstances we think it imperative that you form a limited company.

Case History No. 1

During the preparation for this book we have interviewed many people, who have either started their own business or would like to do so. One of those interviewed is an electrician called Tom. Tom was made redundant just over a year ago. He was at the 'awkward age' — late forties, early fifties and felt fairly sure he would never find another job. The idea of not working again was out of the question so far as Tom was concerned and so with his redundancy money he started a small business, hiring out his skills as a sub-contractor to builders and offering a general house maintenance service direct to the public. Tom has been an electrician all his life and he has never had to deal with paperwork. So, you ask, what were his problems — VAT returns, tax? No none of these.

Tom realised that these were subjects he could not handle and so he simply employed a good accountant and solicitor to deal with them for him. When we met him he had one major problem on his mind. His business was expanding and he needed to take on someone else. A young lad of eighteen had been made redundant at the same time as Tom. They got on well, the boy was a good worker and Tom felt he should offer him a partnership. What was worrying Tom was how to construct a legal partnership, what would happen if the boy wanted to leave, and all the other partnership problems we have discussed in this chapter. Our advice was that in no circumstances should Tom offer the boy a partnership. We understood Tom's requirement, he wanted the boy to feel he was working with him . . . not for him. However the questions we asked were, whose telephone is used for the business, whose van, whose money is being used to pay for promotion, who has the years of experience behind him to talk authoritatively to builders and customers alike? The answer of course is Tom. The business is his and that is the way it should stay. What we suggested is that he paid the boy a fixed salary, but gave him a share of the profits. That way the boy felt part of the business but could leave at any time without causing Tom disruption. Tom took our advice and we hear the 'partnership' is working well.

Case History No. 2

Remember the trials and tribulations of Barbara and Elizabeth in the previous chapter? That story offers a perfect example of the advantages of a limited company. When Barabar left the business if she and Elizabeth had traded through a limited company, it would simply have been a question of reorganising the shareholding. But the business was a partnership and the trauma of splitting it up undoubtedly contributed to its failure. Elizabeth had nothing to offer anyone new — no shareholding or directorship — just the record of a failed partnership.

In a nutshell here is our advice. Whether you set up in business as a sole trader, as a partnership, or as a limited company, keep in the forefront of your mind 'WHAT HAPPENS IF THINGS GO WRONG?'

·Let's face it, if you make a million your worries will be centred round how to spend it! What you have to worry about are the trials and tribulations which will test the structure of your business and believe us, when we say, you are going to have plenty of those on the way to that first million!

9. The Financial Whiz-Kid — That's You!

*Dealing with . . . how to assess and present financial requirements.
How to prepare profit plans and cash forecasts.*

Being in business, especially in the early stages, is all about money. Yes,
of course, you may have this brilliant idea of conquering the world with
your newly invented silent lawn mower, or altering the face of the high
street with your fantastic fast food restaurants. But how much is all this
going to cost, and what sort of profit (if any) is the business going to
make?

Let us take it for granted that you are a good engineer or a competent chef. To set up and run your own business you need to have a proper understanding of the financial implications. Capital is required, profits need to be made and your business needs to be able to 'stay alive' in a cash flow sense while you are doing it. It is vital that you go through a series of basic financial exercises as part of 'getting it together', in order to establish that your project is viable. This, of course, is essential if you are going to borrow money — you must have the right financial tools 'to sell' your project. It is, however, just as important to go through the viability exercise if it is your own money you are going to use. You might well find that the legacy from 'Auntie Maud' would be better employed safely invested, while you sun yourself in the south of France.

Forget for a moment family, partners, bank managers, investment trusts and government grants. If your business goes wrong, their suffering will only be secondary. It is you who will have to bear the brunt of failure, and it is vital, therefore, that you satisfy *yourself* that your project is a winner.

On face value, it would appear difficult to provide you with a formula for establishing business viability which can be applied to every type and size of project. Jim and Harry, setting up in partnership as home decorators, presents a far more straight forward picture than your silent lawn mower project, with its requirement for 70,000 sq. ft. of factory, expensive machine tools, 60 employees, and a marketing budget that would keep Jim and Harry in comfort for the rest of their lives. Surprisingly it does not matter how easy, complicated, big or small the business — the basics are the same. It is as simple as this. You have to sit down and put together a forecast of anticipated sales and costs.

We will try and give you good basic guidelines on how to go about it. Forget the multiplicity of words to describe the process — 'business planning', 'five year budget', 'resource forecasting' — the list is endless. What you are going to produce is a *profit plan*. Both words are important. *Profit* is the reason you are in business. *Plan* means just that — not an optimistic target, not the minimum achieveable if virtually everything goes wrong, not a set of figures pulled out of the air, not what you think your bank manager wants to hear. A profit plan represents your careful assessment of what you reasonably believe will happen — setting natural caution against natural optimism.

The second stage of the operation is to produce a *cash forecast*. Here again we will take you step by step through the exercise, but having satisfied yourself that your project is viable via the profit plan, you must then translate your findings into a cash requirement. You may well be able to convince yourself that by the end of year two, your profits will be substantial, but can you finance yourself (or persuade someone else to) in the meantime?

The Profit Plan

(1) Decide how far ahead you need to go in your planning. One, two or even three years, are reasonable, depending on your circumstances. Less than a year is not enough. More than three years is likely to produce more fiction than fact. We would recommend a year from when you start trading for most businesses.

(2) The first figure you need to work out is what sales you expect to achieve month by month. *This is the most important part of the plan.* You need to know all you can about your product or service, your market, your pricing policy, your production capacity and your means of promotion. You must be confident of your sales projection — it is the key to the plan. How do you go about it? First, you need to decide the price at which you are going to sell your product/s or service. After that you need to estimate how much you will sell each month. You might find that your monthly sales figures can be based on a series of specific orders, or built up around a particular contract. Alternatively you might well be confident of your sales level in, say, six months time, but have to take an intelligent estimate of the figures in the intervening months. You must be confident that your product or service will sell or you would not be going into business in the first place. So with this, as with everything else in your new business, you are going to have to think positive.

(3) Then calculate what your direct costs will be on those sales. If you are manufacturing a product, your direct costs will be raw materials, components, sub-contracted items, and productive labour. If you are merely buying and selling a product, your direct cost will just be your purchase price. If at the other end of the scale you are simply selling your own time, as a technician of some sort, your direct costs will be nil. Many businesses have sales which fall into several categories — an interior decorator will provide a consultancy service with no direct costs, and will also sell furniture, on which will be a buying/selling margin. In these circumstances the sales projections will need to be split down into categories, to identify the direct cost percentage. The difference between the sales figure and your direct costs is the *gross profit*.

(4) Gross Profit is a very important bench mark in most businesses. The gross profit margin can, of course, vary enormously from business to business, but suffice to say that you will generally sleep at night, if your gross profit always exceeds your total overhead! An insurance broker may well need to have a turnover of £40,000 per month to earn £5,000 in commission. By contrast, a retail fashion shop may well turn over as little as £7,000 to earn the same £5,000 gross profit — yes the

margin is far greater, but then so are the overheads in relation to the sales.

(5)   Having projected what sales you will achieve, and how much gross profit they will produce, you then need to work out how much it will cost to run the business. In order to calculate the running costs you must look carefully at the following factors:

(a)   How much space you need.
(b)   How much equipment you require.
(c)   How much indirect labour you need (those people such as secretaries and administrators, not directly involved with production).
(d)   How much your transport will cost.
(e)   How much your administrative costs will be — such as light, heat, telephone, post.
(f)   How much insurance you will need.
(g)   How much your sales expenditure will be — i.e. advertising, promotion and salesmen's expenses.
(h)   How much legal and professional help you will require.
(i)   How much your interest on borrowing will be.
(j)   How much your equipment will depreciate.

And, of course, any other general expenses.

These costs represent your *overheads*. You should calculate them on a month by month basis, and it is important to note that these overheads should be recorded, not as they fall due for payment, but spread over the period to which they are relevant. In other words, to take a simple example, your rent may well be payable quarterly, but you should show the rent allocation for each month, so that the profit calculation for that month can be assessed with its full share of overhead.

(6)   *Net profit*. Having carefully listed the overheads for each month, you should deduct these from the gross profit and the figure left is your net profit, or, if the overheads are higher than your gross profit, the net loss.

John and David's Profit Plan

In order to assist you in producing your own projections, we thought it would be helpful if we plotted the profit plan and cash forecast of a hypothetical business to show you how the picture is built up. Our heroes are John and David. They have decided to get together to make and sell a range of kitchen furniture. John works in the sales department of a large company which produces kitchen furniture as a side line. David has just been made redundant by an office equipment manufacturer, where he was foreman in the furniture factory.

This is the background to their proposed venture:

(a) Both men are very enthusiastic about their project — John is prepared to put £10,000 of family capital into the business. David would like to do the same, but he can only scrape together £5,000.

(b) They have designed a small range of furniture and they expect to be able to sell £10,000 per month.

(c) They need 2,000 sq. ft. of production and office space.

(d) They need £3,000 of equipment in the factory and office, plus a van and a car.

(e) They need initially three people, plus David, in the factory, and someone to help them in the office.

(f) They intend to start the business in January, move into their premises at the end of February, and start production at the end of March.

Here is their profit plan — and some notes on how David and John arrived at these figures:

Sales: John has already the promise of business from his existing contacts, and he expects to take orders from January onwards, for delivery commencing April. David says that he can be in full production by May, but they do not expect to be selling at the rate of £10,000 per month until June. August and December are poor sales months for obvious reasons. See how all these factors have been incorporated in their sales plan. It is imperative that you take seasonal trends into account, and that you allow enough time to establish your business.

Direct manufacturing costs (cost of sales): Careful costing of the furniture indicates that wages (including National Insurance) will work out at 18% of the selling price. To be prudent the plan has allowed 20%. Similarly the cost of raw materials and components have been calculated at 27%, but for safety, a figure of 30% has been used.

Please note that the labour and material figures in the plan each month are not necessarily the amounts actually expended in that month — they are the labour and material costs relevant to the sales made in the month. In May for instance, the business is expected to be in full production, but sales are only £6,000. The balance of production costs have gone into stock. This is inevitable in most manufacturing industries, but do beware of stocking problems. Too much slow moving stock is one of the biggest single causes of business failure.

Overheads: Most of the items of expenditure have been estimated as accurately as possible for the first year of trading, and simply spread over the twelve month period, relatively evenly. As already indicated, for a profit plan, the date of actual expenditure is not relevant. Printing and stationery costs are an example of this treatment. The methods of budgeting for some of the other operating expenses are worth examining

	January	February	March	April	May
Sales				2000	6000
Direct Costs					
Labour 20%				400	1200
Material 30%				600	1800
Gross Profit 50%				1000	3000
Overheads					
Staff Costs					
Wages and Nat. Ins.	1100	1100	1400	900	900
Travel Expenses	50	50	50	50	50
Car Running	200	250	250	250	250
Property Costs					
Rent			400	400	400
Rates			150	150	150
Light and Heat			100	100	50
Repairs and Maintenance			40	40	40
Administration and Sales Exps.					
Printing and Stationery	50	50	50	50	50
Telephone and Post	50	50	100	100	100
Legal and Professional	60	60	60	60	60
Insurance	10	10	30	30	30
General Expenses	20	40	50	80	80
Advertising and Promotion	100	100	100	100	100
Van Running			200	200	200
Finance Costs					
Interest and Bank Charges	10	20	30	40	50
Depreciation			40	40	40
Bad Debts					
Total Overheads	1650	1730	3050	2590	2550
Profit (Loss) — Month	(1650)	(1730)	(3050)	(1590)	450
Cumulative	(1650)	(3380)	(6430)	(8020)	(7570)

KITCHEN FURNITURE   YEAR 1

June	July	August	September	October	November	December	Total
10000	10000	6000	9000	10000	10000	6000	69000
2000	2000	1200	1800	2000	2000	1200	13800
3000	3000	1800	2700	3000	3000	1800	20700
5000	5000	3000	4500	5000	5000	3000	34500
900	900	900	900	1300	1300	1300	12900
50	50	50	50	50	50	50	600
250	250	200	250	250	250	250	2900
400	400	400	400	400	400	400	4000
150	150	150	150	150	150	150	1500
50	50	50	50	100	100	100	750
40	40	40	40	40	40	40	400
50	50	50	50	50	50	50	600
100	100	100	100	100	100	100	1100
60	60	60	60	60	60	60	720
30	30	30	30	30	30	30	320
80	80	80	80	80	80	80	830
			300	1100	100	100	2100
200	200	200	200	200	200	200	2000
70	70	70	70	70	70	70	640
40	40	40	40	40	40	40	400
2470	2470	2420	2770	4020	3020	3020	31760
2530	2530	580	1730	980	1980	(20)	
(5040)	(2510)	(1930)	(200)	780	2760	2740	2740

in more detail. In calculating your overheads it is worthwhile taking plenty of time and really making sure that you cover every possible expense — it is far better at this stage to put in a figure for a possible expense which you may not need rather than run the risk of underestimating your overheads.

Wages, salaries and National Insurance: David and John have agreed that they will each draw a salary of £6,000 for the first year. January, February and March overheads contain these salaries, plus the cost of National Insurance. In March they anticipate being joined by a girl in the office. In April, David's salary comes out of the overheads section of the plan, and is absorbed in the direct labour cost of manufacturing, since he expects to be involved full time in production by then. You will see that the overhead level of wages and salaries continues through to October, at which stage it is assumed an additional person will be employed for sales and administration.

Car running: David and John have decided to lease a car for a three-year period, inclusive of all maintenance costs. This will cost £150 per month, and in addition they have allowed for the estimated cost of petrol and insurance on a monthly basis.

Property costs: As you will see, these are all budgeted to start at the time the premises are to be taken over.

Legal and professional: These costs may look rather high, but we have to take account of the initial opening costs, and an estimate for the annual audit fee — it is assumed that David and John have formed a limited company.

Advertising and promotion: Allowance has been made for the printing and distribution of sales literature, and the estimated costs have been spread over the first few months (which is when the resultant sales will fall). At the end of the year an increased level of expenditure has been assumed, to allow for the cost of attending a local furniture exhibition.

Van running: A small delivery van will be required as soon as production gets under way, and again it has been assumed that this vehicle will be leased.

Interest and bank charges: At the time the profit plan is being pieced together, David and John do not know how much money they will need in addition to their own investment. It is difficult, therefore, to anticipate the interest costs. It is prudent, however, at this stage to have an educated guess and make some allowance for interest. This figure can easily be adjusted once the cash forecast is completed, but if you make some provision now it will ensure that you do not forget this overhead at a later date.

VAT: All sales and cost figures *exclude VAT*. The VAT charge made to customers is simply paid over to the government, less any VAT suffered on purchase of raw materials, equipment and expenses. *VAT, therefore, has no impact on profitability* for a business of this size which has to be registered for VAT.

So what does the profit plan tell us — and David and John. It may well come as a surprise for them to realise that they will lose over £8,000 in the first few months, and that it will take them another six months to recoup that opening loss. More significant, however, the plan demonstrates that they will make a profit in their first year (after paying themselves a proper salary) and once they achieve their expected level of sales, they can look forward to quite a reasonable profit each month. At this stage, it might be sensible to extend the plan for the second year, to see how the figures look. However, even without doing so, it is apparent that with the same set of assumptions, year two will show a profit of between £20,000 and £30,000 — not bad.

Well done David and John — but here is the snag. How much money will they need, and where is it to come from? First things first. Let us take the profit plan and all the assumptions we have made to produce it, and let us construct a cash forecast for the first year. That will show us how much money the business will need.

The Cash Forecast

As with the profit plan, let us look at the way the cash forecast for David and John is produced. The estimating has been done. The cash forecast is something which will flow naturally from the assumptions made in the profit plan. Basically it is a question of taking each item of income and expenditure itemised in the profit plan and judging which month the income will actually come into the bank, and in which month payments will have to be made. Here is the cash forecast together with some comments on its preparation:

Sales: We have assumed that all trading is on monthly credit, so that the initial sales in April are all due for settlement by the end of May. We have also assumed that averagely a fifth of the cash due each month will not in fact be received until the following month — sorry but that's life!

Material purchases: It has been assumed that it will be necessary to hold a stock of raw materials and components sufficient to cover two months production. The initial stock has to be purchased in March and thereafter each month will see the purchase of enough material for one month's production. Because the business is new, with no track record on credit rating, it is anticipated that some suppliers will insist on cash on delivery. It is however considered that 70% of purchases will be settled on normal montly terms.

CASH FORECAST   JOHN AND DAVID

	January	February	March	April	May
Sales — 80%					1600
— 20%					
Receipts					1600
Materials — 30% Cash			1800	900	900
— 70% Credit				4200	2100
Factory Wages — 70% Net				1400	1400
— 30%PAYE/NI					600
Staff Wages — 70% Net	770	770	980	630	630
— 30% PAYE/NI		330	330	420	270
Travel Expenses	50	50	50	50	50
Car Running	720	230	230	230	230
Rent		400	1200		
Rates			150		900
Light and Heat				100	
Repairs and Maintenance			40	40	40
Printing and Stationery		250	50	50	50
Telephone and Post	50	50	50	50	200
Legal and Professional			300		
Insurance				320	
General Expenses	20	40	50	80	80
Advertising and Promotion			500		
Van Running			700	180	180
Interest and Bank Charges			60		
Factory/Office Equipment	1500		1500		
Payments	3110	2120	7990	8650	7630
Net Cash (Out)	(3110)	(2120)	(7990)	(8650)	(6030)
Net Cash In					
Total Cash Requirement	(3110)	(5230)	(13220)	(21870)	(27900)

June	July	August	September	October	November	December	Total
4800	8000	8000	4500	7200	8000	8000	50100
400	1200	2000	2000	1500	1800	2000	10900
5200	9200	10000	6500	8700	9800	10000	61000
900	900	900	900	900	900	900	9900
2100	2100	2100	2100	2100	2100	2100	21000
1400	1400	1400	1400	1400	1400	1400	12600
600	600	600	600	600	600	600	4800
630	630	630	630	910	910	910	9030
270	270	270	270	270	390	390	3480
50	50	50	50	50	50	50	600
230	230	180	230	230	230	230	3200
1200			1200			1200	5200
					900		1950
	200			150			450
40	40	40	40	40	40	40	400
50	50	50	50	50	50	50	750
50	50	200	50	50	200	50	1050
							300
							320
80	80	80	80	80	80	80	830
				1700			2200
180	180	180	180	180	180	180	2320
160			210			210	640
							3000
7940	6780	6680	7990	8710	8030	8390	84020
(2740)			(1490)	(10)			
	2420	3320			1770	1610	
(30640)	(28220)	(24900)	(26390)	(26400)	(24630)	(23020)	(23020)

Wages and salaries: Do not forget that PAYE and National Insurance have to be deducted from staff wages and salaries and remitted the following month to the Collector of Taxes. This effectively spreads about 30% of the gross payroll into the following month.

Car and van running: As explained in preparing the plan, the car and van will be leased. Three months rental will be required in advance when each vehicle is put on the road. In addition, a year's insurance premium will also need to be paid.

Legal and professional: Some costs connected with the start-up of the business will need to be paid at an early stage. Audit and other professional costs may well not need to be paid within the first twelve months.

Factory and office equipment: It is reasonable to allow for payment of 50% with order and the balance on delivery.

VAT: For simplicity, and to enable the figures to be identified more readily with the profit plan, VAT has again been omitted. The effect of VAT on the cash flow in fact will not be significant.

So what do we, David and John, learn from the cash forecast? In the first six months, cash expenditure exceeds cash income every month. This is not surprising. What is surprising, however, is the extent of the net cash outlay — over £30,000 — and it is not difficult to identify the causes:

> Purchase of equipment.
> Initial trading losses.
> Payment of expenses in advance (rent, rates, vehicle leases).
> Purchases of material stock.
> Build up of finished stock in advance of sales.
> Just over one month's credit on sales.

The peak cash requirement occurs at the end of six months, thereafter it seems that normal trading will produce positive cash flow.

What David and John have to decide is how they are going to bridge the gap between the £15,000 they have available and the £30,000 they apparently need. First, they should go through the cash forecast again with a 'fine tooth-comb', especially looking at some of these factors:

> Do they need to purchase equipment for cash, or would HP or leasing be a better alternative?
> Can they somehow cut back on the opening losses?
> Do they really have to hold two months' stock of materials?
> Do they really need to manufacture in advance of order?
> Can they shorten their credit terms with their customers?
> Can they extend their credit terms with their suppliers?
> Do they really need a delivery van?

Let us assume that they feel they should stick to their original plan and the cash flow consequences. They want to press on, and therefore they really have three alternatives:

1. They can put more money into the business themselves.
2. They can find someone to invest some capital.
3. They can acquire a bank loan and/or overdraft.

One thing is certain — they have reached the stage where they will have to sell themselves, and their project, to a backer or banker. Now, armed with their profit plan and cash forecast, they have the tools with which to do so. Losses are acceptable and heavy capital investment is acceptable if both are *planned*. Just supposing for a moment that David and John had not done this exercise. We now know that in month four of their operation they would have already lost £8,000 of their precious initial £15,000 of capital. However, much more significant, we now know that in the same period they would actually have spent nearly £22,000. What do you think their chances would have been of going to see a bank manager and saying "Look we've lost £8,000, we can't pay our creditors, and we need to borrow some money?' Unless he was a very imaginative bank manager he would turn down the project. But David and John know what is going to happen to them in month six, they have planned it. We are absolutely confident that if David and John have the experience their backgrounds indicate and they are enthusiastic and hardworking, not only will they have no real trouble in raising that extra £15,000, *but their business will succeed*.

We will follow John and David in Chapter 10 but before doing so it is worth stressing that preparing a profit plan and cash forecast is neither difficult nor complicated — it is simply common sense. You can easily cope with producing sets of figures just like these — what you cannot cope with is the consequences of not doing so.

Case History No. 1

In 1977, I (Alan) founded a freight forwarding company called Overall Transport with an old colleague of mine, who has been in the freight forwarding business all his working life. We sat down together and constructed a profit plan for three years, which envisaged opening three or four offices within the first few months, and employing twenty to thirty people. The projected loss for the first twelve months was £68,000 but profits were indicated in years two and three. The cash forecast indicated a requirement for peak funding of £113,000 in the thirteenth month of trading. The business was undoubtedly viable. My colleague had impeccable pedigree to run it, but neither he nor I had anything like sufficient capital to finance such a venture.

I decided we needed £60,000 of share capital, plus £60,000 bank facility. We brought in a private investor who contributed part of the initial £60,000 and then armed with that capital base, our profit plan and cash forecast, we went to the bank. Back we came with a £60,000 overdraft facility.

In fact the losses in year one were slightly less than expected, and now, five years later, we have a highly profitable business. Why? We have been lucky, we have worked hard, but the real reason we have succeeded is because we *planned* to do so.

Case History No. 2

A few months ago we met an awfully nice chap in a pub. He was drowning his sorrows, and asked us to join him — it seemed churlish not to do so! After a few drinks, he told us the cause of his sorrows. That day he had appointed a Receiver to his little business. The company would undoubtedly be wound up. He had lost all his money.

Gradually the story unfolded. On the death of an elderly relative, Bernard (our drinking chum) had been left just over £25,000. Most of his working life he had been in advertising and as such had come in constant contact with printers. The printing business had always fascinated him and although he had no formal training, years of buying print had taught him a great deal about the business. His inheritance made up his mind. As he said to us 'Twenty Five Thousand Pounds seemed more than enough to start a little business. I didn't want to found an empire.'

So with his money he acquired a tiny factory and two second hand printing machines. He employed a master printer, who he had known for many years, and an apprentice.

As far as one could judge, from a chance meeting, Bernard is a very likeable fellow, and we are sure he is a good salesman. Everyone worked hard and as the months went by sales began to build, but more slowly perhaps than Bernard had anticipated. Printing machinery is not cheap, nor is employing people, and Bernard had only been in business for five months when he ran out of money. His bank were in fact sympathetic and gave him a small overdraft, but totally insufficient to keep the business afloat while he built up sales. Creditors started pressing. This was month eight and Bernard was out of business.

From a chance meeting in a pub, of course, it is impossible to be certain whether Barnard had the basis of a good business, but we suspect he did. It had just never occurred to him to consider how much money it would take to start his own venture. We would like to bet that if Bernard had put together a proper profit plan and cash forecast, he would probably have needed nearer £50,000 than £25,000. If he had taken his proposal along to his bank before he went into business, we believe his bank manager would have lent him the money.

So many businesses fail through being under-capitalised. Starting a business costs money. You cannot expect to move straight into profit. Losses cost money. Having prepared your profit plan, go over and over it until you are sure you have got it as right as it can be. It is the key to success . . . or failure.

10. 'The Money-Bags' — A Guide to Backers and Bankers

Borrowing money is easy. If you have some of your own it helps, but if you have none at all, it is still possible to borrow sufficient to start a really viable venture.

Ask any would-be entrepreneur why he has not started his own business and he will tell you that he would very much like to but he does not have the money. Money is always put forward as the biggest stumbling block in starting your own business — it is not. The main obstacles along the path to your success are very largely those outlined in the first section of this book. If your project is truly sound and you can demonstrate you know what you are doing, then you will succeed in obtaining the finance.

In this chapter we will take you through the various sources of outside finance, but firstly let us consider *your* position opposite the financing of your business.

If you have money

It may be that you have surplus capital, an inheritance, a nest egg for a rainy day, savings or redundancy money. It may be that you have considerable assets — for example you can borrow money against shares or a first or second mortgage on your house. It may be that you are starting the business with a colleague or partner who has money or a relative or friend is willing to back you.

How much of these existing personal resources you are prepared to commit to your venture depends very much on your attitude of mind. We are taking it for granted that you are convinced of the viability of your business. You do not have to demonstrate this by stretching your personal finances to such an extent that you are worried sick. For example, your project might need £40,000 to launch and run successfully. You may be able to raise £20,000 by a mortgage on your house, in which case your bankers might well be prepared to loan you a further £20,000 against a personal guarantee. The business is yours and yours alone — all the profits are yours — but so are all the worries. There is little value in owning 100% of a business in which the proprietor is in the midst of a major nervous breakdown!

The message here is that just because you have the ability to raise the money personally, it does not mean that you should necessarily do so — it may well be worthwhile involving a partner or financial institution to share the risk.

Although we cannot generalise and tell you what you should do in an investment sense, we can tell you what we would do. If we were launching a project requiring £40,000 and we had all the capital available to us, we would use no more than was required to maintain 100% of the equity of the business. We would borrow the rest. We might even be prepared to part with a minority holding in the business to someone willing to take on most of the financing. We will give you examples on how to do this later in the chapter, but there is a lot to be said for keeping your own personal 'powder dry', so to speak.

If you have no money

If this is the case obviously you are going to have to rely entirely on outside finance. It is possible these days to take a scheme to a bank manager where you require to borrow 100% of the money required and for the bank to help you with the assistance of the Government Guaranteed Loan Scheme — more details on this later in the chapter. It is true to say, however, that in order to persuade a banker to lend you 100% of the finance required, your circumstances have got to be fairly special. You will need to be highly skilled and experienced in the trade of your choice, and your presentation of the facts and figures surrounding your project will need to be highly professional. In other words, you are going to have to work an awful lot harder than the guy with money!

The alternative, of course, if you have no money, is to team up with someone who has. There are tremendous tax advantages these days to anyone investing money in a new business and if you can find the right backer it can be an extremely rewarding relationship. A man who has cash usually has considerable experience in how to acquire it! You may well benefit enormously from his advice. You should aim to strike the right balance in the relationship. Without too much interference, your backer can share in your personal pride and achievement in the growth of your business and gain enormous satisfaction from it. By contrast, investments in the stock market are awfully dull.

So, if you have no money, but a really sound idea, read on . . . there are ways and means . . .

A Guide to outside finance

These are the options open to you for the finance of your business:
  (1) *Investment by an individual*, either in the form of capital or loans.
  (2) *'Institutional' investment* (from organisations such as ICFC) again by a combination of capital and loan facilities.
  (3) *Bank loans and overdrafts*.
  (4) *Grants, loans and assistance from Government* or 'official' sources — organisations such as CoSIRA, The Department of Industry and Local Authorities.
  (5) *Payment of the 'Enterprise Allowance'* for up to one year to help unemployed people start their own business.
  (6) *Hire purchase or leasing* of plant, equipment, or vehicles.
  (7) *Rental of property* rather than purchase.
  (8) *Factoring of debts*.
  (9) *Loans against endowment and pension policies*.
  (10) *Loans from suppliers* within specialist industries.

Any of the above categories of financing might be suitable for you, or more likely a combination of several. First, we will explore each category in greater depth and then give you some examples as to how these various forms of financing can be combined to give you the sort of package you require.

Individual investment
Having found your backer, provided he sets up the investment properly, he can offset the entire amount against his income for tax purposes. If, for example, he is putting £10,000 into your project, up to £7,500 will be

paid for by the Inland Revenue — quite a significant reduction in his commitment and risk.

But where do you find this mythical character, you ask? Who is going to act as your own personal Father Christmas? Both your accountant and solicitor will have clients who pay high rates of tax and are willing to invest in new business ventures. Alternatively, think of the contacts within your own trade. Supposing, for example, you have worked for a company for a number of years. but have been made redundant. If you are starting your business in a similar trade, think about the suppliers you dealt with over the years. They know you, they know you have a good knowledge of the trade — they might well be prepared to make some form of investment in your new venture — particularly if at the same time they are developing a new customer!

If none of these sources are forthcoming, you are going to have to keep talking. You are enthusiastic about your project — talk to friends, relatives, people you meet in the local pub. Cast your net as wide as you can. If your project is a good one, someone, somewhere is going to help you.

If you draw a complete blank with all your contacts, you could try taking an advertisement in the financial column of a newspaper. Quite honestly, it is not something we would highly recommend, but if you really do have no alternative, it is worth giving it a try. It is a waste of time advertising locally — your best chance of finding a backer is to advertise in the *Financial Times*.

In your search for a backer do not become despondent. When you find him do not feel that it is he who is doing all the favours. The opportunity to invest in a viable business venture should be attractive, stimulating and lucrative.

'Institutional' investment
This means money borrowed from such sources as pension funds, insurance companies, and merchant banks. The problem is that these organisations are generally not geared to helping the small business. You have to boast a turnover of at least £100,000 a year, and in many cases considerably more, to even approach them. Their main investments are usually in large well-established companies.

The exception to the rule is ICFC (*Industrial and Commercial Finance Corporation*). ICFC was founded by the major clearing banks and the Bank of England, although it is an independant commercial body. Its sole aim is to provide finance for the establishment, growth and development of small and medium-sized businesses and it is very keen to get involved right from the birth of a business.

ICFC will offer loans from as little as five thousand pounds up to two million pounds. Its staff are easy to talk to and they realise the importance of the founder of the business being in control of his company. In other words, they are not greedy in their requirement for equity — ICFC usually only take a minority holding. In addition, they will not interfere with the running of your business, particularly if it is a small one. The ICFC head office is in London at 91 Waterloo Road, London, SE1 8XP, but it has local offices in many of the major cities round the country.

Bank loans and overdrafts

On the one hand we are told that banks are in business to lend money — on the other hand we are told that you have to have money to borrow it! Both views are true — up to a point.

A popular misconception in approaching a bank is the assumption that banks will provide the permanent capital for a new business. This really is not the function of a bank. The bank's job is to support your day-to-day trading, usually by means of an overdraft facility, or to loan you money for a specific project — such as the purchase of a property, plant or equipment.

The most common form of funding for a small business is an overdraft facility. The main advantage of an overdraft is that, unlike a fixed loan, your borrowing will fluctuate according to the requirements of your business. Interest is usually calculated at between two and three per cent over bank base rate, so it is not cheap, but it does give you that much needed degree of flexibility.

The disadvantage of an overdraft facility is that it is rather insecure. Normally facilities are granted for a twelve-month period and are subject to review. It can be very nerve wracking. A poor year's trading or a new branch manager (or worse still, both!) can give you a few sleepless nights leading up to the review date. Assuming you can convince your bank that your business is still healthy, no bank manager is going to seriously alter the basis of your borrowing to the extent that it will put you out of business. You will still worry though!

As already indicated, bank loans are normally granted for a specific purpose. You might well find, in the establishment of your business, that your bank offer a mix of facilities — a bank loan to finance the purchase of equipment and an overdraft to cope with your day-to-day trading.

It is difficult to summarise what you can expect a bank to do. However if you or your partner are putting some money into the business, a bank will usually be prepared to match it by lending you a similar amount. The bank will almost certainly require a charge on the assets of the business and your personal guarantee. You may need to support your guarantee by a charge on your personal assets.

Having said that, new banking horizons have been opened up recently in two different ways. First, a number of the banks have introduced specific schemes to provide virtually all of the initial finance for a new venture by way of medium term loans. The *Business Start Loan Scheme* operated by Barclays Bank is a good example. They charge a royalty on sales instead of charging interest, and they do not require personal guarantees. The second new area has been established by the introduction of the *Government Guaranteed Loan Scheme*, which makes bank borrowing altogether more acceptable to the small businessman. Supposing you take a proposal to a bank to borrow £20,000. The bank manager may feel that it is not really a banking proposition, because you are unable to provide adequate personal guarantees, you have no track record and very little personal money to invest. If he feels the project is a viable one, he can apply, on your behalf, for the Government Guaranteed Loan Scheme. What this means is that the Government guarantees 80% of your loan, so that in the event of a default on your part, the bank is only liable for 20%. We have talked to a number of bankers about this scheme, and apparently it is working very well indeed.

Finally there is the question of selecting your bank. As with professional help, do not be afraid to shop around. As a general rule we have always found that if your borrowing requirement is small, you would do best to go to your own local bank manager. His local knowledge can be very helpful. However, if your borrowing is large, we do recommend that you go to a major branch. The larger the branch, the larger the manager's personal discretion when it comes to the amount of money he is authorised to lend. By far the best way to sell your project is to sell it to the man who is going to make the decision. If the bank manager cannot make the decision himself, he then has to put your project up to his regional office. A second-hand sales pitch can never be as effective. Also there is the human element. Yes, bank managers are human! A man at a major branch will be used to handling large borrowings, whereas a requirement for £20,000 in a small market town would be far more daunting.

Grants, loans and assistance from Government or official sources

There are a whole range of measures designed to provide 'official' backing for new ventures specifically and small businesses generally. The Government do have millions of pounds available for this purpose and the money being offered comes in the form either of cash grants or loans — usually at a special low rate of interest. In particular the Government is anxious to promote industrial expansion in so-called 'development areas'. Certainly, if you are living in one of these areas, your chances of receiving financial help are fairly high. There is a mass of legislation and a profusion of schemes available and it is difficult to sort out the wheat from the chaff.

If you live in a small town or rural area you should contact CoSIRA (*The Council for Small Industries in Rural Areas*). They are a very nice bunch of people. As well as making available small cash loans and grants, they can be terribly helpful in giving you advice on a range of subjects — from marketing your product to setting up an accounts system. Their head office is Queens House, Fish Row, Salisbury, Wiltshire, SP1 1EX.

Similar regional bodies to CoSIRA are the Welsh Development Office, the Scottish Development Office, The Highlands and Islands Development Board, and the Northern Ireland Development Office. Then there are the Regional Development Boards, and a number of Local Authorities now also advance money for specific projects.

Your bank manager, solicitor, or accountant, should be able to guide you through the wealth of schemes available, or you can contact the *Small Firms Division of the Department of Industry*. Their address is Abell House, John Islip Street, London, SW1, telephone number 01-212 3395. The Department of Industry has a number of regional offices — their London office will advise you of your nearest.

Because of the complications surrounding Government aid, you can be forgiven for feeling an appalling sense of lethargy when it comes to tackling the red tape. However, grit your teeth — these schemes are well worth pursuing. Remember, if you are lucky enough to obtain a grant, it is free money! Even if you receive a Government loan, the interest rates are always considerably better than you would be charged by a bank or an institution such as ICFC.

The Enterprise Allowance
We mentioned this allowance in an earlier chapter, and it is a good scheme. If you have been continuously unemployed for three months or more, you can apply for a weekly allowance, which will be paid to you for a year while you establish your own business. Full details of this scheme are available from your local Job Centre.

Hire purchase or leasing
This is expensive, but there are grounds for saying that sometimes it is advisable not to have all your financial eggs in one basket. If, for example, you have a fairly hefty overdraft with your bank, you would probably rather not approach them for a loan for equipment as well. We do feel it is preferable for you to have financial aid from several sources, rather than from one — it gives you a much greater degree of flexibility — and in this respect hire purchase is very useful.

Let us explore the case for leasing as against outright cash or hire purchase. If you need a piece of equipment which you are going to use constantly, day in, day out, it may well be worth while your looking at leasing. To give you a personal example, we both drive somewhere between 40,000 and 50,000 miles a year. It is far better for us to lease a car than it would be to buy the vehicle. We lease for a three-year period, and let's face it, what car is worth very much after 150,000 miles of heavy motoring? If, however, the piece of equipment you require is only going to have moderate use and is something that will not require constant updating, then it would be better to buy. An example of this is the fork lift truck we bought for our freight forwarding company. It cost £12,000. A fork lift truck is essential, but it is only used once or twice a day. It will last for years and in these circumstances it is better to buy.

Whether you are taking on a leasing or hire purchase commitment, do check the agreements very carefully. Yes, we know they look like a standard form but they are not always, and if you have any doubts, do check with your solicitor before signing anything.

Rental of property, rather than purchase
Assuming yours is not a business which can be operated from your back room, you are going to require premises. Most new businesses start by renting their premises, and on the whole we would recommend this. The problem is that if you are just starting up you may well experience difficulty in taking a lease of a property. Even small units until recently, have often been out of reach of the new business because the proprietors could not provide adequate references to the developer — in property jargon 'their covenant was not good enough'. However, many Local Authorities are now recognising this problem and are taking head leases from the developers and then renting the individual units on short term tenancies to small local traders. This is enormously helpful to the small business and it is well worthwhile asking your Local Authority if they have such a scheme.

Of course the initial funding of your business could be linked to the purchase of a freehold property. The problem with the early acquisition of a freehold is that in addition to stretching you financially, you may find that the property you have bought is not suitable for your business in the long term. Despite careful planning you may well find that your business develops much faster, or slower, than you anticipate, and in our view it is far better to let the development side of the business settle down before you start buying property.

Factoring of Debts
Debt factoring represents very useful working capital support for a going

concern. Every time you raise a sales invoice for goods or services, the factoring company effectively buys the debt, paying you 80% of the amount due immediately and the other 20% when the customer settles his invoice. The factoring company will actually take over your sales ledger administration, collect all your debts for you and will give you credit insurance. Factoring has the major attraction of turning your sales into cash very quickly. It is more expensive than borrowing from the bank because you pay interest on the money you are using, plus an administration fee.

As indicated, however, the problem with factoring is that it is not available until you are properly established in business. Factoring companies like to see you with well established sales and a fairly substantial number of invoices going out each month, before it is worthwhile their becoming involved. Factoring companies will not help if you are trading direct with the public — factoring is essentially designed to cover commercial transactions.

So do not look to factoring as an immediate means to financing your business, but once you are established, have a talk to your bank manager and he will advise you as to the best company to use if you wish to pursue the matter.

Loans against endowment and pension policies
This again is a form of funding available only to established and essentially profitable businesses. Once you have a reasonable profit record, you may be able to introduce a pension and life assurance scheme. The premiums are charged against the business profits, and an endowment policy is created to provide immediate life cover and a retirement pension. A loan is then taken out from your bank or from the insurance company against the security of the policy, the money being put into the business to support future growth and development. You need to talk to an insurance broker specializing in life and pension business. This is a complex subject and your accountant should be involved in any discussions because you need to be sure of the tax implications.

Suppliers' loans
Certain specialist industries receive considerable funding from their suppliers. The two major examples of this are probably public houses and garages. If you buy a pub, and are prepared to sell the products of just one brewery, that brewery may well be prepared to give you financial aid. This may take the form of a straightforward loan. More often, the brewery will provide the money to refurbish the bar, build on a restaurant, increase the size of the car parking — indeed anything which they can see will increase sales of their beer.

Garages and pubs are the prime examples of large scale financial aid, but you may well find, on a smaller scale, that there are all sorts of deals you can do with suppliers. Here is another example. I (Deborah) used to manufacture childrens' clothes. Most of the garments we made had popper fastenings, since these are easiest and safest for children. I agreed to purchase my popper fastenings from just one company, in return for which they loaned me, free of charge, initially one, and eventually six, machines for applying the poppers. These machines would have cost several thousand pounds if I had needed to buy them. Look out for these sort of deals. They can save you a lot of money.

So we have outlined for you the main ways of funding your business. Detailed below are a few examples of the type of financial packages you could well put together and which are likely to be acceptable to all the parties involved.

Example No. 1

Let us go back to our friends David and John and their kitchen furniture business. If you remember they had £15,000 between them and their cash forecast indicated that they had a requirement for £31,000 — say £35,000. So they need to find £20,000 of financial backing.

In these circumstances, it is quite likely that a bank would not be prepared to commit £20,000 even with personal guarantees. Two ways in which David and John would be most likely to raise the money are as follows:

(i) They could find a private investor to put £10,000 into their business for a 40% stake. Armed with their own £15,000 plus a further £10,000 from Mr X, they could approach their bank and in our view would be granted an overdraft facility of a further £10,000. The bank most likely would require a debenture (charge) on the assets of the company, but would be unlikely to require personal guarantees.

(ii) Alternatively David and John could approach ICFC. We feel that they would put in £5,000 capital for a 20% stake, plus an additional £5,000 loan. Again armed with £10,000 from ICFC, plus their own £15,000, the partners could approach the bank for an overdraft of £10,000. In these circumstances, the bank and ICFC, would probably require a joint debenture, and because the bank would only have security on half the assets of the company, it is likely that they would require personal guarantees.

One of the problems that David and John face in approaching a bank is that the money they require is largely to finance initial losses, debtors

69

and some stock. In time they will build up assets. However, starting from scratch, if things went wrong, the bank is going to find it very difficult to get its money back. In a case where more secure assets are involved, the bank is likely to take a different attitude.

Example No. 2

Let us say a printer decides to set up in business and requires £25,000 which would largely be required for equipment. The printer in question can put up £5,000 of capital and he has his own home which is worth much more than the amount of his mortgage.

In these circumstances we suspect that a bank would be prepared to loan the printer £15,000 over a ten-year period and give him a working capital facility of £5,000. In return the bank would take a debenture on the assets of the business and would require a personal guarantee from the printer, supported by a second mortgage on his house. You can see the bank's point of view. If things go wrong, they will have a prior claim against the assets of the business including, of course, the valuable equipment. If the business assets do not realise enough to discharge the bank borrowing, they also have the security of the printer's house.

Example No. 3

Supposing the same printer had no capital and no house as security and he still required £25,000. This would not be a normal banking proposition, but under the Government Guaranteed Loan Scheme, the bank should be able to offer a similar deal — say, a bank loan of £20,000 over ten years and a bank overdraft of £5,000. But in this case, 80% would be guaranteed by the Government. To be eligible for the scheme, the printer would have to be a qualified man with several years experience in the trade . . . but then we would recommend he was anyway before embarking on such a project.

So far we have been talking about fairly large sums of money. Smaller sums can be easier to acquire but so much depends on your type of trade.

Example No. 4

Supposing you were setting up as a cabinet maker, requiring five thousand pounds, with a thousand pounds of your own money. Assuming you did not live in a large city you could approach CoSIRA, who would most probably give you a loan of £2,000 over seven years to purchase equipment, (if could be a grant, depending on Government attitude at the time). Armed with £2,000 from CoSIRA and £1,000 of your own money, you could approach your bank and would most likely be granted a loan, or overdraft for a further £2,000, possibly even without the necessity for a personal guarantee.

If you had no money at all, and were living in the city, you could not apply to CoSIRA. However, the bank might well fund you the full £5,000 under the Government Guaranteed Loan Scheme.

The cabinet maker is getting a sympathetic hearing because he is manufacturing in this country. In time he may take on staff — the Government see him as an investment in Britain's future.

Example No. 5

Supposing instead of starting up as a cabinet maker, you came back from an Italian holiday inspired with the idea of importing leather belts. Again, you feel you need £5,000. In these circumstances there is no chance of a loan from CoSIRA and it is much less likely that you would get a sympathetic hearing under the Government Guaranteed Loan Scheme. Your only chance would be to obtain a firm order from a large reputable company, against which your bank would probably advance you the money to purchase your belts. Alternatively, you might obtain credit from your Italian supplier, though this is unlikely.

This might seem a rather prejudiced attitude, but all backers and bankers alike are encouraged to support British industry, rather than sheer speculation.

As we have indicated, a mixture of financing is a good idea. We are involved with a manufacturing company. The company had a turnover slightly in excess of one million pounds when the present directors funded its purchase from an international parent company, by a personal bank borrowing of £20,000. In addition, they retained a £200,000 mortgage loan provided by the original owners. They secured a day-to-day overdraft facility of £50,000 supported by a floating charge on the assets of the company. They then embarked on a development programme, the increased trading levels being funded by debt factoring, which at any one time can be up to £150,000. All major equipment was purchased on HP, totalling £40,000. They have ten cars and several commercial vehicles on lease, the capital cost of which is over £50,000.

The directors are currently negotiating to replace the £200,000 vendor mortgage by a long term loan from an insurance company, secured against a newly introduced pension policy.

It is a careful mix but it works, and the company has never had cash flow problems. It makes money too!

Presenting your Case

We have spent a considerable amount of time talking to backers and bankers about what makes them accept, or reject a financial proposal. It is quite clear that although the content of any proposal must be sound, many people fail, not because there is anything wrong with their proposed venture, they just do not know how to present it. Here are a few hints which we have picked up along the way:

(1) *Be prepared* — In addition to taking your profit plan and cash forecast with you, also take the evidence to back up your figures. Your prospective backer will be primarily interested in your sales projections where possible provide orders, enquiries, contracts, or if you have none of these, a market survey. Almost the first question you will be asked is how your sales forecast is calculated — you must know the answer! Include also with your package any property valuations on the assets, or any independent report you may have. Certainly, if you can obtain a letter from your Regional Development Board, CoSIRA, or some such body, pledging support and confirming the viability of the project, this will help enormously. With all documentation, take along the original but have a copy ready to leave with your backer or banker.

NB If you have had some professional help with putting together your cash forecast and profit plan, do make sure you understand the figures. A marvellous presentation will be ruined if you are floored by the questions you are asked.

(2) *If it will help, take along your partner, your accountant or solicitor* (remember their fees!) but only do so if you feel it will aid your cause. Too many people putting across their point of view can be confusing.

(3) *Do not worry if you are turned down, and do not be afraid to shop around.* I (Deborah) had a very interesting piece of advice from CoSIRA when I started in business. The CoSIRA accountants helped me to put together a cash forecast and profit plan and we decided on the bank to whom I should make my presentation. I had never asked a bank for money before and naturally felt somewhat nervous. The advice from CoSIRA was brilliantly simple. They suggested that I did not go to the bank of my choice first, but tried out my presentation on several other bank

managers. How right they were. I was turned down by the first two bank managers I approached, but as my presentation performance improved, I gained in confidence. When I finally made my presentation to the bank of my choice it was accepted. If you are turned down by a backer or banker, for goodness sake learn from it. Before leaving, ask them *why*. The reason they have turned you down might be something you cannot alter, but at least when you come to make your next presentation you can change the emphasise and hopefully lead the attention away from what you know to be a problem area!

(4) *If you do have your proposal turned down several times, whatever you do keep the date on your presentation documents current.* This is a very good tip we received from one of our friendly bank managers. He said that the first thing he did when he started to look at the documentation provided was to check the date. If it was, say, September and the documents were all dated July, he knew that several people had turned the project down before him. In these circumstances a bank manager cannot help but be influenced by former banks' rejections. Obviously he is going to be more critical. It sounds obvious doesn't it, but as he said, 'you would be amazed how many people do not think this one out'.

(5) *In our view it is terribly important to establish a good relationship with your backer or banker.* Actively seek his advice and listen to what he has to say. Mutual trust and respect is what you should be building towards.

So there you have it, a resumé of the various methods of financing your business. It is an absolute maze but we can only stress again that if your project is a good one, you will find a way. Always remember, however, that borrowing money is expensive. Too much expansion, too fast, can put you in a position where you are having to make enormous profits just to pay your interest bills. It can quite easily reach a point where you feel you are working flat out for your bankers and backers, rather than for yourself. Make sure that in all your financing dealings it is the dog who is wagging the tail.

11. 'The Professionals'

Dealing with . . . a guide to accountants, solicitors, insurance brokers, estate agents and consultants — are they a help or an expensive luxury?

Professional advisers are going to play an important part in the establishment and growth of your business — particularly solicitors and accountants. However modest your venture, you are going to require their help from time to time. Many people feel there is some sort of mystique attached to the member of a professional body. These are feelings you must dispel — you should go shopping for professional help, in much the same way as you would for any other commodity. You are looking for the right product at the right price to suit your particular needs.

Whatever the profession, you need to seek a firm which is appropriate, as far as possible, to your immediate requirements. If you are borrowing half a million pounds, employing a hundred people, and renting 50,000 sq. ft. of warehouse space, then you should approach the largest firm in your area, since they will have sufficiently large resources to cope with your various requirements.

However, most of us starting out in business do not begin on such a grand scale. As a brand new small company you approach, say, a very large firm of accountants. After the initial interview with a partner, you will get fobbed off with an articled clerk, to deal with you on a day-to-day basis. You do not want this. You want to find a small firm to whom your business is important.

In looking for professional help, therefore, first consider the locality. Time is money. Try and find a firm close to your premises, to avoid your travelling far. Second, as always, do not be influenced by personal relationships. Do not approach a firm simply because one of the partners happens to be married to your wife's best friend! The very best way to find the right firm is to ask advice from other businesses in your area, of the same sort of size as you intend to be. Another useful source of information is your bank manager, if he is a local man. Third, it is important that you both instinctively like, and trust, your professional advisers. Many solicitors and accountants particularly, can exude an air of gloom and pessimism which you can well do without. They can be so pompous — you can do without that too! You are looking for someone who is bright, intelligent, courteous and interested in what you are doing. He should be a person who gets thing done — so many professional bodies seem to think that time and deadlines apply to other people, but never to them.

Remember who is employing whom. You are paying the piper — you call the tune.

A Guide to Accountants

However small your business, as a general rule we do recommend the services of an accountant. As a self-employed freelance person, you can have a direct relationship with the Inspector of Taxes, and annually provide him with a full schedule of your income and outgoings so that he can assess your taxable earnings. However, unless you are very experienced in tax affairs, even if you prepare your own return, we do suggest that you at least talk it through with an accountant. Tax men can be very helpful, but they may not give you all the advice you need. Accountants are paid to do it.

The other point is that although you may have a very small business, with very simple accounts, which you should in theory well be able to handle yourself, you may be the sort of person who is somewhat chaotic with figurework. Have a good, hard look at yourself. If you are not a numerate person, who finds figurework easy, it is well worthwhile paying an annual fee to have all the worry and headache taken off your shoulders. You can use the extra time you have available to concentrate on working on the things you are good at, you enjoy, and which make you money.

If you are forming a partnership, it is imperative that you employ a firm of accountants to produce an annual set of partnership accounts. Any share of profits must be made with reference to a full set of audited accounts, and as mentioned in Chapter 8, this is a clause which should be incorporated into any partnership agreement.

If you are forming a limited company then legally you have to have your company's books audited once a year by an established firm of accountants.

We have shown you how to prepare a profit plan and cash forecast and in Chapter 13 we will advise you on the preparation of management accounts, to help you keep track of how your business is developing. If, however, you are in the high risk business (big turnover and small profit margin) and you or your staff cannot produce management figures, we would advise that you consider employing an accountant to produce monthly management accounts. It is no good reaching the end of your financial year and then finding you have made a crashing loss. In these circumstances the information will arrive just in time to coincide with your going out of business. If you are making losses you need to know quickly so that you can do something about it.

If you are wishing to borrow a fairly substantial sum of money from your bank or a financial institution, in our view it would be worthwhile employing an accountant to help you prepare your profit plan and cash forecast. In some instances, it would probably be helpful to ask your accountant to come with you when you make your proposal. This can prove an excellent plan of attack — you can dazzle the bank manager with the brilliance of your project, while your accountant is 'talking his language' and putting up a good case for why the bank is not going to lose its money if they back you!

Just two notes of caution on the subject of accountants.

(1) There are a number of people around who call themselves accountants and who are not qualified. These people usually operate on their own. If you are uncertain you can easily check whether your man is

qualified — he should either be a Member of the Institute of Chartered Accountants, or the Association of Certified and Corporate Accountants. If he is not, do not hire him.

(2) Accountants are expensive. Do as much of the spade work for them as you possibly can. It is terribly important that you always keep proper records of your business activities, for your own sake. Also, do remember that the more work you do in keeping complete and accurate records, the cheaper your accountant's bill. Before seeing your accountant always work out exactly what you want him to do and give him clear and precise instructions — preferably in writing. Make sure you provide him with all the information he is going to need.

It is impossible to generalise and give you any clear indication as to what sort of fee you should expect to have to pay. Some firms of accountants may suggest that you pay them a monthly retainer, for which they will handle all your business requirements. We would not recommend this — certainly in the early days. Many firms bill quarterly in arrears (on a time basis) for the work they have done, which is preferable.

A Guide to Solicitors

As already indicated, if you are entering into a partnership we strongly advise you to employ the services of a solicitor. In the formation of a limited company also, in our view, it is imperative. If you are a sole trader you may well feel that it is not necessary for you to have a solicitor, but in the development of almost any business, from time to time, you will need legal advice. It may be because you are acquiring a property, suing a customer for a bad debt, or being sued for bad workmanship. We would advise that as a general rule, if you are going into business on your own, you need to establish a relationship with a local solicitor who is aware of you and the structure of your business, whose advice you can seek as and when you need him.

Again, legal advice is not cheap. Solicitors mostly charge for every telephone call they make and every letter they write — it soon mounts up. You might find it tremendous therapy to talk through your business problems with your solicitor every few weeks, but can you afford it? Having said that, we feel that your solicitor is probably more likely to be your mentor when it comes to advice, than your accountant. Solicitors on the whole are less cautious than accountants, and more inclined to state their opinion. They are more likely to encourage you with your expansion plans and help you seek new opportunities. In addition, solicitors have to cope with every problem known to man — that is their

job. However severe your problems, never be afraid to disclose all to your solicitor. Odds are he has heard it all before.

A Guide to Insurance Brokers

If you are an electrician setting up a freelance business, you probably think this section does not apply to you — it does. You are in business now. Insurance rules are quite different. First, your transport. O.K., so you are going to use your own car, but you are going to use it for business purposes now and you need a brand new policy. A crash could put you out of business if you are not properly covered.

Let us pursue the hypothetical case of the electrician for a moment. He goes to mend the toaster of a customer, he is tired, accidentally he mixes up the wires and half an hour after he has gone, while Mrs. Bloggs is using the toaster, the cable explodes and gives her a severe burn. She has a very good claim against our friend the electrician, which could wipe out his business overnight. *If you are providing any form of service or product, you must have public liability insurance cover.*

After a few months, our friendly electrician is doing well and decides to employ a mate. Even if it is on a part-time basis, he will require employers liability. Once he has staff he will also need to ensure he has public liability cover for them — in case his mate blows someone up!

It sounds both complicated and expensive doesn't it? It can be. For this reason we suggest you employ an insurance broker — it is far better than going direct to an insurance company. You do not pay the insurance broker. He receives a commission from whichever insurance company he uses on your behalf. He is not employed by any of them, which means he is free to shop around for the best possible deal. As with all the other professional bodies, the best way to find your insurance broker is through personal recommendation.

A Guide to Estate Agents

So you want premises? If so, go and find them for yourself. If you employ a firm of estate agents to find premises for you, they are going to charge you a fee. In addition — and you may have had this experience when looking for a house — they also sometimes seem incapable of assimilating your requirements and acting accordingly. If you require a 2,000 sq. ft. warehouse for light industrial use, they are quite capable of sending you to a 30,000 sq. ft. office block.

It is going to take time and give you sore feet, but visit all the estate agents in your area and keep checking their books until a suitable property emerges. Also keep your eyes open. Over the years we have found several properties simply by noticing that an old barn or warehouse is empty, and making enquiries to find the owner. This is particularly likely to happen where you require a property simply for warehousing. Do remember, however, that if you are going to carry on

any form of business activity you must very carefully check that you have planning permission. This equally applies whether you are acquiring a property through an estate agent or not. On the whole, Planning Authorities are bending over backwards these days to help small businessmen get established, but they get very angry indeed if you do not ask their permission first!

A Guide to Consultants

We do not like the word consultant very much. May be it is just because it begins with a letter 'C' but it always makes us think of con-men. There are an awful lot of people around at the moment, particularly with such high unemployment, who have set themselves up as management consultants, marketing consultants, business consultants — the list is endless. It would be quite wrong to dismiss everyone who calls himself a consultant. *However, when you start your business, if you have a good bank manager, a good accountant, a good solicitor, and a good insurance broker, you do not need a consultant.*

As your business grows, and your responsibilities increase, you will have to start carefully managing your time so that you use it properly. In these circumstances, there are occasions where a consultant could help. Consultants can be helpful, for instance, if you intend to make a major purchase. One of our businesses recently bought a computer. I (Alan), although an accountant for many years, have to admit to a very limited knowledge of computers. Any good computer salesman could make absolute mincemeat of me! Therefore we employed the services of a computer consultant, who thoroughly assessed the requirements of our company and then found the right product to suit our needs. These tactics could equally well apply if you are buying any large piece of equipment, which requires a considerable capital outlay and takes you into a field where you are not an expert. For example, a surveyor is a consultant and you would not dream of buying a house without employing one, would you?

A Question of Balance

We are not going to quote you case histories in this chapter because there are too many to choose from! Wonderful stories of professional advisers seeing fantastic opportunities for their client's businesses, turning small, barely profitable companies into great profit earners! Similarly there are horror stories of legal wrangles, insurance claims, and companies failing through bad advice.

It is a question of balance. Your professional advisors are not there to make policy decisions for you. You should not use them as a crutch to avoid facing up to your responsibilities. It is expensive apart from anything else.

The professionals are there to smooth your path along the way — to advise and guide in areas where they are expert. As with all advice you receive, however, a note of caution — retain in your mind the ability to stand back and do a quick critical appraisal of what you are being told. The best advice you will ever receive is from your own sense of native cunning.

12. The Team

Dealing with . . . staff — the pros and cons of being 'the boss'.

If you have the choice between hiring a man or machine . . . hire the machine. It is a terrible thing to say in the teeth of so much unemployment, but do not start taking on staff unless you absolutely have to . . . but if you do have to, get it right.

There is much evidence to support the view that once you start employing people, your troubles really begin. Against that people make a business — people *are* the business. Your venture is a viable one — a good salesman will sell your products, a good production manager will see your customers get their orders on time, a good accounts clerk will see you get paid. Employ the wrong people and what few orders you do get will be delivered late, so what chance have you got of getting paid? What price your viable venture now? Few people manage to run a business without any help even if they start it with one or more partners. So let us go through the process of employment step-by-step, towards building your Team.

The Decision

So you have decided you need staff. As indicated at the beginning of this chapter, the first part of your thinking process should be whether the job could equally well be done by the acquisition of more sophisticated equipment. Let us give you an example. We had lunch the other day with a married couple who run their own public relations company. Their business is doing well, and they are taking on more and more clients. For some time now they have been considering the wisdom of employing a secretary to relieve the wife, Veronica, from doing all the typing. When we had our lunch they had made their decision, and they were well pleased with it. Instead of employing a secretary they had bought an extremely sophisticated typewriter, which doubled as a word processor. The cost of the machine was nearly £2,000 but as they pointed out, the monthly HP commitment was considerably less than a secretary's wages and after three years the machine was theirs.

The second aspect you should consider is whether your requirement for staff is a continuous one. Taking again the example of secretarial help, do you really need a large quantity of letters typed every day? If the answer is no, you would be far better using the services of a freelance typist. There are plenty of agencies and individuals who will provide this service. And what applies to typing, applies to many other business services. Just one note of caution on freelance help, however. It is not a clever way to get round employing full time staff. If over a period you employ someone continuously, in a freelance capacity, they can claim an employment relationship.

Third, as part of the decision process, do make sure you identify whether the position you wish to fill is a permanent one. In other words, if you are taking on a couple of extra chaps in the work shop because you have just landed a large contract, what is going to happen when that contract is completed? Hiring them is easy, firing them is not. Far better, in those circumstances to employ them on a fixed contract basis. If your business prospers, you may well be able to offer them long term employment. If, however, work is slack, at least at the end of the contract you have no commitments to them.

Recruitment

Having identified that you have a requirement to employ staff, what is the best method of finding them? It is surprising that even with today's high unemployment figures, finding the right person for the job is not easy, as any personnel officer could confirm in a more candid moment. To be honest, we do not like employment agencies any more than we like estate agents! They are fiendishly expensive (most employment agencies charge you at least two weeks salary for filling a vacancy, and in some cases much more). Also, like estate agents, they do seem to find it difficult to correctly interpret your requirements. We can both honestly say that neither of us have ever found an employment agency who have thoroughly interviewed applicants before sending them along. We are sure there must be some good agencies . . . somewhere! Instead we favour the Job Centre for manual and clerical workers (it's free!), and an advertisement in your local paper for more senior posts.

You do have to be careful with advertisements. Here are a few points to consider when advertising:

(i)   You must take care not to infringe either the Sex Discrimination Act, or the Race Relations Act.

(ii) The wording of the advertisement is very important. Keep it simple — quote the basic job description and details such as location, age of person required and salary, if you are prepared to disclose it. Be specific — if, for example, the applicant must be able to drive, say so. It can save you hours of sifting through useless applications. Clear and concise details describing the person you require saves everyone time and trouble.

(iii) We do not recommend display advertising in local papers. It really is not necessary, and just costs extra money. People looking for a job read small print and we would venture to suggest that your money would be better spent running the advertisement for a second week, to give you a wider cross-section of choice. You might be looking to fill a very big management post and are perhaps advertising nationally. There are grounds then perhaps for saying that a display advertisement might be justified in order to attract someone who is currently employed. As a general rule, however, it is a waste of money.

(iv) Take advice from the advertising manager of your local paper as to which are the best days for advertising job recruitment.

(v)   Unless you are in a tremendous hurry to fill the job, and have a secretary who can handle telephone calls, do not quote your telephone number in the advertisement. If your advertisement is any good you will spend your whole day answering the telephone instead of getting on with running your business! Ask applicants to write in.

Interviewing

Firstly you need to carefully read your written applications. Quite a number of these you will be able to turn down immediately because they are obviously unsuitable. Then it is a question of interviewing the rest and producing a short list. We can hear you groaning — yes it is a time-consuming business, but well worthwhile doing properly. You may have someone within your business who can do the short listing for you. During a period that I (Deborah) was recruiting a large number of staff, my secretary, Diana, used to short list down to six applicants for me to see. She was so much more qualified than someone from an employment agency. She knew the job, she knew my company, she knew well the people with whom the new applicant would have to work, and she knew me!

Volumes have been written about interview technique. We always feel that the best results are obtained by making the interview as relaxed and informal as possible. Of course you want to make sure that the applicant understands the nature of your business and the vacancy available, but mostly you want the applicant to do the talking. I am sure many of you will have been for interviews where your prospective boss hardly draws breath in expounding the virtues of his company. He then asks you half a dozen standard questions and you leave wondering how on earth he can judge you from any of the other applicants. So get your applicants talking. If they are any good you will find out. If they are not, they will trip themselves up!

Listen closely to their track record. Constant changes of job can be a bad sign. Be cautious too about people willing to take a drop in salary. In these difficult times it may not be sinister, but it is worth checking out. Another indicator to watch for, is if the applicant speaks ill of his current or ex-employer, or is quite willing to leave his current employment without proper notice. If he can behave like a rat to his former employer, he can behave like a rat to you. Whatever you do, do not glamourise the job. If anything, make it sound worse than it is!

Finally do ask for, and take up, references. We suggest that you make your reference checks by telephone. You will get a much clearer idea of what the referee really thinks over the telephone, rather than just rely on the usual standard letter.

Hiring

Having made your decision, it is important that the new recruit is issued with a contract of employment, if he or she is going to work for you for more than 16 hours per week. This contract of employment can well take the form of an exchange of letters. It simply needs to state all the details of employment:

The rate of pay.
Whether it is paid weekly or monthly.
Normal hours of work.
Holidays and holiday pay.
Provision for sick pay.
Pension schemes, if any.
The job title.
Starting date.
Notice required by both parties.

Once you start employing people, you need to be familiar with the methods of calculating PAYE, National Insurance and Sick Pay, and you must keep proper wages records. It is not difficult, but it is time consuming. Before recruiting staff, go and see your local DHSS and Tax Office, who will provide you with the paperwork you need, and will explain to you what is required. It is important that you fully understand what is involved before you start hiring staff.

How to be a great leader

Possibly the best known philosophy which has issued from the lips of many a desperate boss is 'if you want a thing done properly, do it yourself'. But just like the bad workman who blames his tools, ineffective staff usually mean an ineffective boss. If you are inexperienced in employing people, you are likely to fall into one of two traps. You may well expect too much of your staff. It is easy to be critical if they do not do things your way, but people need time to adjust to a new job. Too much responsibility, too quickly, can ruin a relationship between a man and his boss, and only leads to resentment and usually poor workmanship.

The other major fault of the first time employer is exactly the opposite — his inability to delegate. What is the point of keeping a dog and barking yourself? Maybe you can do the job better than the chap you are employing, but you have other things to do. Develop his skill as far as you can and then let him get on with it. If your business is to expand, it can only do so by delegation. You must know when to let go of the reins.

Running a happy ship is not easy. It is difficult sometimes to be sympathetic over some staff squabble when you are battling away, just trying to keep your business alive. It is very important that you show genuine interest and concern — and it is as important to praise good work as it is to moan when it is poor.

After you have run your own company for a little while, it becomes increasingly difficult to remember what it was like to be employed. Particularly in these hard times, staff do feel very insecure. We have always believed that it is terribly important to keep all your staff fully informed. If your company is going through a good period, get all your staff together and show them the rising graph. Give them a bonus — the more unexpected it is, the better for staff relations! When things are tough going, do not leave them to speculate as to whether they are going to be made redundant the following week. Keep them fully informed as to exactly what is going on. Rumours and gossip are not only usually inaccurate and damaging to the atmosphere of a company, they waste time as well.

Set a good example. You cannot expect your staff to work hard if you are not prepared to. Do not arrive late in the morning. Do not take three-hour lunches. It all sounds rather like being a parent doesn't it? Indeed it is — the joys and sorrows come in about the same proportions. Be good to your staff and your staff will be good to you.

Promotion

We are including here a special section on promotion, because it can prove to be a vital factor in the development of your business. As we have said, people are the business — the wrong people in the wrong job can bring a business to its knees. Everyone, and this includes you, has an optimum level of skill, and ability to take responsibility, above which he or she cannot go. You start your business from scratch, employing one or two people, who work round the clock to help you get off the ground. Your natural inclination, as the business starts to grow, is to reward them for the loyalty and hard work. Your instincts are right, but it is all too easy for these rewards to take the form of over-promotion beyond your staff's ability.

Let us give you an example. I (Deborah) started a cottage industry 10 years ago. In the early days, I employed two or three women who worked hard taking orders, packing, sweeping the workshop floor, whatever was required. Let us follow the career of one of these women, Anne, who started working for me as an order clerk. It meant she opened the post every day, sorted out the orders, banked the cheques, and carefully recorded customer requirements. Anne was excellent at her job. Four years later, she ran a department of five girls doing this same job. Her responsibilities were no longer to sit there filing orders, but to see that five other people did it effectively. Anne just was not up to it, and it caused a great deal of distress all round. I should have had more sense. As the business started to grow I should have recognised the point at which I needed to employ a supervisor, senior to my loyal order clerk. Looking back, if I had explained the position to her, she would have understood, but my gratitude to her for her loyal service made me feel it was impossible to bring someone in over her head.

This sort of situation can very easily develop within a small business. One of our colleagues was involved in a large company, which, in his view, went bankrupt through the managing director's loyalty to his staff. The business became a million-pound company but the founder was still employing staff in senior positions who were really only suitable for launching a small business.

We are not suggesting you use people and throw them away. What we are saying is that as your business starts to grow you need to ensure that you are employing the right calibre of people — too many indians can be just as dangerous as too many chiefs!

Firing

Employ in haste, repent at leisure! Hiring is easy, firing is difficult.

Dismissal
The legislation surrounding dismissal has to be treated with respect. Many companies fall foul of the section relating to unfair dismissal. Every member of your staff, part-timers or otherwise, who have been with you for 52 weeks (2 years in the case of a business employing less than 20 people) or more, must be given a written statement of your reason for dismissing him or her. If you wish to dismiss somebody who has been with you for more than a year (or 2 years, whichever is applicable), you should give them three written warnings. These warnings should clearly state your reasons for reprimand, what the employee must do to put things right, and what will happen if he or she does not conform. After three written warnings, he or she may be dismissed, but will be at liberty to take the case to an industrial tribunal, to establish whether the grounds for dismissal were reasonable.

Industrial tribunals have become somewhat more flexible than perhaps they were in the past. They do, for example, now take into account the size of an employer. If an employee is dismissed because he is unsuitable for a job, the industrial tribunal might say that a large company should make strenuous efforts to re-employ him elsewhere in the company. So far as a small company is concerned, it is understood that this may well not be possible.

It is difficult to generalise as to when you can and cannot dismiss someone. What is important is that you make the dismissal procedure as watertight as possible, and certainly if you are a little unsure as to the merits of a particular employee, it is important to make a decision on his future within the first twelve months (two years) of employment, so if you do decide to dismiss him there are no repercussions.

Redundancy

Redundancy occurs when a job ceases to exist. You cannot make somebody redundant one week and then employ somebody else in a similar capacity the following week. Redundancy usually occurs when a company is cutting back through financial strain, but it may also be necessary if a company is genuinely changing the direction of its trade, and therefore requires a different type of employee. An employee is entitled to redundancy pay based on a formula relating to length of service and rate of pay, and is only entitled to redundancy if he has been employed continuously by you for two years or more. Approximately half of the redundancy payments you make are recoverable from the Department of Employment, who should be notified of anybody you intend to make redundant.

Maternity Leave

There are considerable hazards in employing women of child-bearing age. Provided a woman works until eleven weeks before her confinement, and has been continuously employed by your business for two years or more, she is entitled to take forty weeks off and then return to her original job, without loss of seniority at the end of that time. She is also entitled to nine-tenths of her normal salary, less NI Maternity Allowance for the first six weeks of her absence, though the employer can recover the money from the Department of Employment. This legislation does not apply to small businesses employing five people or less.

In general terms you do have to be extremely careful in all areas of dismissal. A case going against you could be absolutely ruinous to your business, since compensation awards can be quite high. Make sure you are meticulous in your dealings in both hiring and firing, and if you have any doubts at all, consult your solicitor before taking action.

We have not made employing people sound much fun. It is enormously satisfying to feel that through your own strenuous efforts, you are able to provide employment. Building your business as a shared experience is very rewarding. The legislation surrounding the protection of employees is obviously necessary, and as long as you stick to the rules, then you should be in no danger.

Look after your Team as you would your family — the people you employ should feel that they are working *with* you, not *for* you. There is a lot to be said for the good old British Team Spirit — it can build you a business.

Case History No. 1

Peter, a friend of ours was looking for a business opportunity a few years ago. He found a small manufacturing company on the outskirts of Birmingham, which belonged to a big group, and which had the distinction of consistently losing £50,000 per year! Peter came to see us full of excitement, 'I am going to buy it,' he said. 'There is nothing wrong with the company, it makes a good product at the right price. It's the people causing the trouble. They are all in the wrong jobs.' To be frank, we both thought he was nuts!

Three months later the company was his. The big group had been quite willing to part with it — it had been a running sore for years, and they thought he was nuts too!

Peter started by firing the managing director. He had already established that the production manager brought most of the sales into the company, so Peter promoted him to sales director, and reorganised the production department. In fact he turned the company upside down! The product remained the same, the pricing structure remained much the same, and the company broke even in its first full year under the new management. Today, three years later, it is anticipated that it will make a profit of £80,000. It is a classic case — starting your own business is not just a question of how you do it — but with whom you do it.

'Doing it'

Getting it together is one thing, actually doing it is quite another.

The day you first unlock the door of your garden shed, or come to that, your 50,000 sq. ft. warehouse, the day you sit down at your workbench or desk for the first time as your own boss, is a day you will never forget. It is exciting, it is challenging . . . it is terrifying.

This next section of the book is concerned not so much with running your own business, as starting to run your own business — from setting up proper administrative systems, to guide lines for marketing and selling your product or service.

So you have your finance and your premises, you know what you want to achieve and what you have to achieve. In other words, you are ready to go. Right — let's get on with it . . .

13.   How to market and sell . . .

We have said it before, but we will say it again — it does not matter how good your product or service, its ultimate success depends on your ability to market and sell it. If you cannot do this yourself then you must find someone who can.

Let us define, first of all what we mean by the terms 'marketing' and 'selling'.

Marketing

Marketing is really a three tier operation.
Phase 1 is all about defining your market. You need to establish where you should sell, to whom, at what price, when, and in what sort of quantity.
Phase 2 is having established your market, deciding how you are going to reach it — your channels of distribution.
Phase 3 provides a backup to the selling effort. Having established your market and started to sell to it, you need to be constantly aware of changes and developments so that your sales (and, if applicable, production) reflect market trends.

Selling

Selling is just that. It is a question of going out there and persuading people that they want what you have got.

Selling a Product

It is very difficult for us to be too specific when it comes to offering advice on marketing and selling, but we will try and categorise the various options open to you. If you are setting up as a manufacturer you will probably not be looking to sell your product to the end user. If this is the case, there are four main channels of distribution for your goods. These are:

Retailing
Wholesaling
Industrial distribution
Mail order

Let us take these areas one by one.

Retailing

You need to accept that if you are going to sell your product to a retailer it is a very time-consuming business. Your business may be a small one — say, making pottery mugs, which you sell to the local gift shop. Even in these circumstances, with just one sales outlet, you will be surprised how much time it takes to collect orders, rejects and money, and to service the customer with sufficient frequency to ensure he does not place his orders elsewhere. Apply this to a slightly larger manufacturing unit requiring to sell to six or eight outlets, and suddenly you find that you need a full-time man doing nothing else — perhaps travelling miles just to pick up a small order, or chase a cheque. It really can be an extremely costly business.

On the face of it, selling to retail outlets direct seems a good idea — it does mean cutting out the middle man — i.e. the wholesaler, which in turn should mean more profit for you. It just is not that easy. If you have a quality product you probably dream of seeing it on the counter at Harrods or Fortnum & Masons. If you have a product you can mass produce, you can probably see yourself selling thousands to a large chain store. If you believe you have a product which has appeal to the large retailer, unless you have considerable marketing experience, do not attempt to sell it yourself — get an agent. Big retail outlets do not respond well to amateur marketing, you do need the contacts in the trade to really obtain results.

By contrast, if you are selling to small retail outlets, you can approach them yourself — in fact small shops respond well to regular friendly service. A note of caution however — small retail businesses are very prone to bankruptcy. So often they are started by amateurs who buy too much of the wrong stock. So if you do start selling your products to small shops, be very stringent about credit control. Never deliver new stock until you have collected all your money from the previous delivery, and right from the outset be very clear as to how much credit you are prepared to give.

Wholesaling

A wholesaler is someone who stands between the manufacturer and the retailer. If you forté is manufacturing rather than marketing, then your best bet is to sell to a wholesaler. No, you will not make anything like the profit you would if you sold direct to a retailer, or indeed direct to the public, but nor will you incur the expenses. When one considers the cost of putting a representative on the road (more of this later) there is a lot to be said for concentrating on manufacturing and employing someone else to do your selling.

Industrial Distribution

As the name suggests, like the wholesaler, industrial distributors stand between the manufacturer and the consumer. In some industries there are both. Like the wholesaler, they are professional marketing organisations, and you will find details in your trade magazine. Both wholesalers and industrial distributors really are essential if you are selling manufactured goods in certain specialist industries.

Mail Order

Selling to a mail order company is a good idea and can be an excellent way to build your business. However, a word of caution. If you think your product is suitable for selling to a mail order company there are several questions you need to ask yourself first.

   (a) Can you turn round your product in a maximum of four weeks — in other words, can you manufacture it from start to finish, including the acquisition of raw materials, within a four-week period? If the answer is no, then there is no point in applying to a mail order catalogue. You must have this facility.
   (b) Is your product easily transportable by post? This is not simply a question of weight, or whether the article is fragile. You must also consider what the product will look like when it has been in the mail for a week. Can you present it in such a way that it will not arrive looking crushed and tatty?
   (c) Your product needs flair — it needs to be a little bit different. Mail order buyers get offered the same things over and over again, and they are always looking for inspiration. Whilst their businesses are not built on way-out merchandise, something classic, with a new twist to it, has the greatest appeal.
   (d) Your pricing needs to be extremely competitive. Mail order buyers are 'red hot' when it comes to knowing their market. They know exactly what everything costs and how much they should pay for it.

You do not need to be a professional salesman to sell to mail order buyers, and they are usually fairly accessible, though do ring up for an appointment first. Remember too that mail order companies work a long time ahead and are very seasonal. As a rough guide, they work twelve months ahead and normally select their merchandise twice a year in April and September.

Selling a Service

If you are not selling a product, you are probably selling a service. If so, you do need contacts. Whether as a freelance architect, artist, photographer, journalist, builder, cook, secretary — the list is endless — it is not just a question of what you know, but who you know. You *can* advertise and you may receive the odd enquiry, but establishing yourself in business is all about making personal contacts.

Remember, the only thing you have to sell is your time, and therefore you have got to make sure that your time is spent as effectively as possible.

There is a lot to be said for offering freelance services. To begin with, it is something you can do part-time while retaining your existing job, so do this, if possible. Freelance service can be established with very few overheads and it is much easier to control growth and development than in many businesses. In other words, you can build the business to the point where you are fully employed and then hold it at that level, or you can continue expanding by sub-contracting the work until you have a sizeable concern. The secret to successful freelancing is to be selective about your work. Do the jobs which pay well and pay on time, which will enhance your standing in the trade and develop your contacts. Don't mess around!

Selling Direct to the Consumer

Whether you are selling your own product or someone else's you can, of course, leap straight to the end of the chain and sell direct to the consumer. You can do this in two ways. Either by retailing or mail order.

Retailing

Retailing means selling direct to the consumer and by definition, therefore, you need to like people. The public at large can be an awfully tiresome bunch. It is impossible to please all the people all the time, and goodness, don't they make sure you know it! Even if your aim is to build up a chain of shops and you feel that you will be more involved with management than working behind the counter, you still need to be able to understand your customer. How else are you going to train your staff?

Let us look at the conventional shop first. So you decide you are going to open a book shop. You see a dear little premises that looks just right, but how do you know it is? In retailing there is only one really important issue — Conrad Hilton, the famous hotelier, summed it up. When asked what the three most important factors were in siting a business, serving the public, his answer was, 'location, location and location'. So scour the neighbourhood, see what competition there is — if down the road there are a couple of local newsagents with big book departments, you are probably wasting your time. Retailing, however, is a strange thing. In many towns and cities you will probably have noticed whole groups of antique shops in one street. Similarly, in a tiny country village, perhaps sporting a population of four hundred, you will find two first-class pubs, both with Haut Cuisine restaurants. There are many examples like this which can best be described as 'parasite marketing'. An area becomes established as the place to go to buy 'X' and you simply jump on the bandwagon. In general terms, however, we believe as Conrad Hilton does — find the right location and the rest will follow.

There are, of course, many forms of retailing. If you are a craftsman, with proper planning permission you can open your workshop to the public. Not only do they have the thrill of watching you work, but it saves you the expense of having to employ someone to sell for you. Factory sales are another good idea. You can get together a range of goods (we are told they need to be in the under £10 bracket) and visit large factories on pay-day. Many big companies will allow you to set up your wares and sell to workers in their lunch break. Which brings us to market stalls. Many famous retail chains began on the market stall. As a form of retailing it is not to be despised. There is many a market stall that takes a great deal more money in one day than a high street shop does in a week, with, of course, a fraction of the overheads.

Selling to the consumer is demanding and exacting, but if you like people, and above all have the imagination to anticipate their requirements, it can be very rewarding.

Mail Order and Direct Mail
This is a very specialist field which attracts a great many amateurs, with often disastrous results. The terms are easily confused.

Mail order is the sale of goods direct to the customer through general press advertising. *Direct mail* involves sending direct to the home of potential customers a brochure or sales letter to generate a sale.

Whether you are manufacturing or buying-in a product, it is often believed that mail order is an easy way to sell — it is not. You need to appreciate the enormous number of people you will have to mail to acquire a reasonable-sized response. In direct mail, with well established customers, an acceptable result for a mailing is a sales response of somewhere between 4% and 7%. In mail order, you will be very lucky indeed if you get a response in the region of 0.25% of the circulation of the newspaper or magazine. In both cases if you get your marketing wrong, it can be considerably less than that. We would strongly recommend if you are considering mail order, to join a mail order company for a few months to learn the ropes. If you do not do this, at least employ the services of an advertising agency to help you — not any advertising agency, an agency specialising in mail order.

Salesmen and Agents

We are not very much in favour of small and medium-sized companies employing salesmen, unless they really have no alternative. For every one salesman worth his salt, there are several hundred who are nothing but expensive luxuries. Consider the costs. They usually require a basic salary, plus commission, plus expenses, plus a car. Putting a salesman on the road these days can easily cost you £20,000 per year. Are you prepared to pay that before you start making money?

If you *have* to employ a salesman, go for the very best. Choose someone who is not too young, and who has had a considerable number of years experience in your trade. Offer him a great big fat commission and a tiny salary, or preferably no salary at all. If he is not prepared to accept this, you have lost nothing because he does not have faith in your product. If your product is good and he is as experienced as he says he is, with as many contacts as he says he has, he will jump at a huge commission. The message, therefore, for employing salesmen is:

(a) don't.

(b) if you have to — buy nothing but the best.

Agents are a good idea for the small business. An agent is a man with a specialist knowledge of a particular trade. He has good contacts with potential customers, and he offers these contacts a range of products from a number of companies whom he represents. He normally works on commission only and supplies his own office and car. A good agent, like a good representative, in our view will not be particularly young. He needs to have built up the experience. If he knows his trade, however, he should be able to place your goods for you with no up-front commitment on your part.

To summarise this chapter, we are asking you to carefully consider whether you have marketing skills or not. Most people find it difficult to combine manufacturing and marketing. If your forté is really that of a manufacturer, then sub-contract the marketing and selling of your products to a professional. If your forté is marketing and selling, then sub-contract the manufacture (if applicable) to a professional. Either way, make sure your profit margins are large enough — whether it is to give sufficient incentive to your selling agents, or to absorb the true costs of doing the job yourself. You are not Superman — you cannot do everything, but what you do, do well.

Case History on a Professional Sales Agent

Last year, I (Deborah) was commissioned to buy knitwear for a large mail order company. Knitwear is not something I know a great deal about and so, on recommendation, I employed the services of an agent based in Leicester. We met in his office, and having explained to him carefully the type of garments I required, he suggested that he should drive me round to the various factories he had selected.

We walked down to the car park and I was absolutely astounded to be helped into the front seat of a spanking new Rolls Bentley. Knowing that knitwear manufacturers very often operate in a tin shed, demonstrating few financial resources, I queried with him the wisdom of driving round to see these factories in his Bentley. 'It works like a charm,' said John. 'I have bought this car with my agency fees, because I sell a hell of a lot of garments. The manufacturers know it and therefore, know I will do well for them. You, the customer, know it and therefore assume, rightly, that I am successful at what I do.' He is a nice guy. We spent a pleasant day, the manufacturers obviously liked him, and I found exactly what I wanted. It was only when I was driving home that evening that I realised I had spent an absolute fortune with him!

You need a chap just like John doing your selling.

14. How to Advertise

We have very little faith in the value of advertising for the small business. It is very expensive and the beneifts are so intangible. There are three exceptions. First, if you are going into mail order, naturally advertising is an integral part of your trade. Second, a retail outlet serving the public may benefit from a little initial advertising to attract additional customers other than purely passing trade. Third, advertising may be justified as a brand awareness exercise, once your business is established and substantial.

However for most businesses, what we are really saying is do not look on advertising as part of your main sales drive.

For most small businesses advertising means taking space in either their trade paper or a local paper. The success of such advertising really has to be judged on three levels.

(1) *The initial response* — i.e. the number of enquiries you receive as a result of the advertisement, which should very roughly represent about 0.2% of the circulation of the publication.

(2) *How many of those enquiries actually turn into orders.* The answer can quite easily be none.

(3) *Having assessed the orders you have received as a direct result of advertising, what is their worth, opposite what it has cost you to obtain them?*

In the vast majority of cases, the answer will be that the cost of advertising is far too high in relation to the number of orders you receive. This sort of experience is especially damaging if you have assumed that your advertising programme will make an important contribution towards your selling effort. If you must advertise, do at least consider the spend as 'mad' money and in no way slacken your sales approaches in other ways.

One of the forms of 'advertising' we do recommend to the small business is a sales leaflet explaining the virtues of your product or service. Whether it is sent out in response to much-maligned advertising, enclosed with sales letters, handed out by sales representatives, or from the bar of the local pub, its aim should be not only to advise people of what you do, but also to reflect the way you do it — i.e. your image. When it comes to producing a leaflet of this sort, do not employ the services of an advertising agent or design studio. They are so expensive and although the results will look slick, the brochure is also likely to be characterless — just like the millions before it, and the millions yet to be printed. Instead, get together with a good jobbing printer, work out what you want to say and get him to lay it out nicely for you. The result will be a brochure that tells the world about you and your business, not how good your local advertising agency is at copy writing.

This leads us neatly to advertising agents. They are nice people, multi-talented, friendly and enthusiastic. They are also very dangerous. It is part of their job to work up enormous enthusiasm for clients and their projects and on the whole they do this without discriminating between the good, the bad and the indifferent. Everything you suggest is 'magic'! By the time an advertising agent has finished eulogising about you and your little business, you can hardly recognise either yourself or it! Statistics and layouts flash before your eyes, pretty girls bring you enormous gins and tonics, while you sit with a dazed expression, surrounded by the standard-issue rubber plants — essential to every advertising business. Seriously, if you wish to launch an advertising campaign, which involves a considerable spend, you must employ the services of an advertising agent for the best possible results. But if you are simply toying with the idea of spending a few hundred pounds, steer clear. Before you know where you are, the heady atmosphere will lead you into commitments you neither want nor need. I (Deborah) have worked with advertising agents most of my working life. I have met good ones and bad ones, and have both been impressed by what they can do and depressed by how much they cost. However, the best ad man I have ever met has an office at the wrong end of Holborn, in a dingy basement. He serves you coffee out of a cracked mug, instead of gin and tonic, and there is not a rubber plant to be seen. He spends more time telling you not to advertise than to spend money with him, and even more extraordinary, he actually tells his clients when he thinks they are doing something wrong! He is a rare bird indeed.

If you wish to find a good advertising agency contact Creative Handbook Ltd., 100 St. Martin's Lane, London, WC2N 4A2, 01-379 7399. They have agencies listed regionally.

To summarise, therefore, in response to this chapter heading 'How to Advertise', our basic answer is *don't*. If you feel you must try it, have a very gentle dabble and do not expect any sales as a result. If you intend to spend real money advertising then employ an advertising agent (and, again shop around for the right one). Keep your head, and never believe your own advertising campaign!

Case History of an Enthusiastic Ad. Man

A short while ago, I (Deborah) was involved in a fashion photography session. I was there representing the client. Also present was the photographer, the model and a representative from the client's advertising agents. We were photographing a model standing against a white-washed wall, and having taken a couple of test shots, we were looking at the results before going into the final shoot. Just beside the model's head, there was a flaw in the wall, where a screw had been. 'Just move a couple of inches to the left,' I said, to the model, 'to cover up that hole in the wall.' Quick as a flash, up jumps the ad. man, a pioneer light in his eye, full of enthusiasm. 'There's no need for that,' he said, 'with our modern equipment we can remove that mark at the reproduction stage'. Bless his heart he meant well, but moving the model a few inches to the left cost nothing. Removing the mark from the photograph to my certain knowledge would cost somewhere between £60 and £100. Ad. men just do not think like that, but then it is not their money they are spending . . . is it?

15. How not to advertise — the benefit of Public Relations

The best sort of publicity is the kind someone else pays for! If you wish to promote your product or service, but you neither want nor can afford an advertising budget, then what you need is a spot of public relations.

Public relations is much misunderstood. As a business function it is placed fairly low on the priority list and is looked on more as window dressing than a serious contribution to the development of a business.

Public relations is simply a question of persuading the media to tell the world that you, your product, or your service, are wonderful. So how do you go about it? It is easy.

Assuming you are a small company, just setting up, the best form of publicity is local publicity. By local publicity we are not simply talking about local newspapers. Approach too your local television and radio stations who really do reach a great many people. The popular misconception is that journalists are remote people, utterly unobtainable and unapproachable. This is not the case. If you have a good story to tell, the average journalist is thrilled to bits! Except on very large national newspapers, most journalists spend a great deal of time looking desperately for stories to fill their space allocation. A ready made story landed on their lap is a Godsend. This brings us on to the question of the presentation of your story.

Most local newspapers, radio and television, do not have the money or staff to send out a reporter and a photographer on every job they do. If, for example, you are opening a restaurant, compose a press release to your local newspaper. This simply means typing an information sheet on your headed notepaper, giving all the details in note form, which you think would be of interest. Preferably enclose with your press release some black and white photographs. These could be, for instance, photographs of the restaurant entrance, or guests enjoying a meal, or the staff. The advantage of having a photograph included with your write-up is that obviously, if printed, it will have much greater impact on the page. In other words do as much of the journalists' work for them as you can.

Bear in mind that a newspaper office is a busy place, which has to react fast to news and trends. If, following the same example, you wish to promote the launch of your restaurant, do not send in your press release twenty-four hours before your restaurant opens. Instead, submit the press release about a week before the opening date, but write the words 'embargoed until 24th August' or whatever the date is. In this way the newspaper or magazine can plan ahead to include it for the day you open.

Where local media is concerned, do try and make friends with the journalists. Journalists are a nice bunch of people, but they do have to be very careful who they promote. If you can build up their confidence — proving you look after your customers and provide value for money, then they will be only too happy to help you on a regular basis with your development. Back to the restaurant — having written an article on the opening you can then regularly supply your local newspaper with information as to special functions and events, and as your business develops, you can probably persuade them to do an editorial feature on 'a day in the life of your restaurant'.

We imagine you will be aware that there are public relations consultants, who will handle for you your promotion through the media. Certainly, if your product or service becomes available nationally it is worth considering a national PR campaign, in which case, it is the stage at which you need PR consultants. Apart from straight forward press coverage there are so many other PR activities — sponsorship, celebrity appearances, press parties, public speaking, and so on, all designed to help promote who you are and what you do. There are a large number of public relations consultants. For full details contact:

The Institute of Public Relations,
1 Great James Street,
London, W.C.1.
Telephone: 01-405 5505

who will be able to give you a list of PR consultants in your area. Alternatively, all reputable PR consultants are contained in a directory called The Hollis Press & Public Relations Annual, Contact House, Sunbury-on-Thames, T16 5HG, telephone 093 27 84781. Like everyone else, public relations consultants vary, but many do specialise in a particular type of business. Certainly if you are speaking to the Institute, it would be a good idea to ask their advice, not only as to the public relations companies in your area, but also the type of business they service best. The normal way to deal with a public relations company is to pay them a monthly retainer, plus expenses. On the face of it, this may seem expensive, but it shrivels into insignificance compared with the average advertising budget. What is important, is that if you employ a consultant you get the very most out of them. Here are a few pointers:

(1) Do keep your PR Consultants fully informed as to your company's activities. A small technological development, which you consider to be of minor importance, your PR Consultants might well be able to blow up into a major newspaper story. Their interpretation of the day-to-day events in the development of your company, will be entirely different to your own. They are the experts and they are looking for news value.

(2) Service your public relations consultants well. Journalists always operate to amazing deadlines. Your consultants can be pursuing a magazine or newspaper for months, in order to get a story printed, and nothing happens. Then one Friday afternoon, at 4 o'clock, the newspaper will ring up and say they must have a black and white photograph of your premises by 9 o'clock on Monday morning. If you do not deliver the photograph by then, two things will happen — first, you will not get your story, and second, you will make it a great deal more difficult for your PR consultants to approach that particular newspaper again. The deadlines to which the press work may be irritating, but it is all par for the course. If you do not like playing the game their way then you should not be playing it at all.

(3) If you are embarking on a serious PR campaign make sure that

either you or your consultant take out a press clipping service. The obvious aim of a PR campaign is to persuade the people who actually read the newspaper or hear you on radio or television to buy your product or service. However, there is also a tremendous spin off advantage in using your newspaper clippings or video tapes to help sell your business concept to new customers or potential investors. You must have a nicely presented press cutting book for this purpose.

The most important aspect of public relations is this — if you take out advertising space, not only is it expensive, but basically *you* are telling the world how wonderful you are. If you obtain editorial coverage in the same newspaper, *someone else* is telling the world how wonderful you are. The difference is enormously significant. Editorial coverage carries far more weight, far more authority than any advertisement, however cleverly worded . . . and don't forget . . . it's free!

Case History

I (Deborah) conceived the idea of starting a children's clothes mail order business in rather a strange way. One early morning in February, I was sitting with my one-year-old daughter on a Norfolk beach. Not surprisingly my daughter was cold, damp and fretful. I was just about to get up and walk back to the little cottage we had rented when I saw a fishing boat coming in. The seas were rough, the boat had to approach the beach at high speed, and at the last minute the fishermen had to hurl themselves over the side into the icy water, dragging the boat to safety. My daughter and I watched fascinated and it was only as the fishermen started to drag their boat up the beach that I realised that they were neither cold, nor wet, nor fretful! Why? They were all dressed in oilskin dungarees.

I looked from my daughter to the fishermen, and back again. It was the obvious answer for small children — little waterproof dungarees that would keep them warm and dry when they sat in puddles, fell over in the wet grass — windproof too. I soon discovered that no other company was making such a garment and so I started making them, and selling by mail order.

You may have read the story — over a period it appeared in most national newspapers and magazines. I mention it because it is not a particularly unusual tale, but it appealed to journalists on a national scale. It demonstrates that you do not need to have revolutionised the world with some amazing technical breakthrough in order to obtain coverage — you just need a good yarn!

16. How to keep control

Keeping control is a combination of systems, people and attitudes.

Book-keeping is a chore in most small businesses, but it has to be done. In fact we would go as far as to say that you cannot have a responsible attitude towards your business unless you keep adequate records.

We hope we persuaded you in Chapter 9 that you do not need to be a chartered accountant to prepare a profit plan and cash forecast. Likewise, you do not need to be particularly numerate, in order to understand and introduce basic simple book-keeping and control systems. Book-keeping really falls into two categories:

(a) the requirements of the outside world; and,
(b) those internal controls which you need for your own benefit to manage your business.

In dealing with the outside world you will need records for:

The bank
Your customers
Your suppliers
The VAT man
The tax man — both PAYE and business tax
The DHSS — both National Insurance and Statutory Sick Pay

The records you require for internal use will cover the following:

Stock control
Costing
Performance — this means keeping track of departments, contracts, debtors, bank overdraft, and of course, most important of all, profit and loss.

In this chapter we are not attempting to take you through the details of double entry book-keeping in any depth. Our companion book in the series *Accounting for the small businesses* will give you all the details you require. What follows are a few thoughts on the basic principles of control. Let us look first at accounting for your dealings with the outside world, under the headings we have already detailed.

The Bank

To keep control of your bank balance it is essential that you have a cash book which records on one side the receipts, and on the other the payments you make. The cash book should be kept up-to-date every day — in other words, you must enter the cheques drawn and the takings as they occur. At least every month you must check these against your bank statement and reconcile the bank statement against your cash book balance. Ask for weekly bank statements — they help you keep control. Routine is what you need. You, or someone in your office, should provide you with a bank balance every Monday morning and you should never go home until that cash book is written up!

Customers

If you sell on credit terms, but only raise a few invoices each month, you can keep track of outstanding accounts by keeping a file of unpaid copy invoices in your top drawer. When you get the cash in, bank the money, enter the receipt in the cash book and place the invoice in the file of paid invoices, in your bottom drawer.

If you produce any real volume of sales invoices you need a sales journal to list, total and analyse your sales, and a sales ledger to record the sales to each customer. We will talk about invoicing and debt collecting in rather more detail in Chapter 18, but would stress at this stage how absolutely vital it is for you to invoice promptly, as soon as the goods or services are supplied — not at the end of the month! You cannot afford to give anyone extra credit so remember to send out statements within a week of the end of each month. You, or someone in your office, must produce a list of debtors at the end of each month, with outstanding balances listed according to age. Outstanding debts need your personal attention.

Suppliers

As with sales invoices, if you have only a few purchase invoices each month, files in your top and bottom drawer work well! Otherwise you need a purchase journal and a purchase ledger. The purchase ledger should be kept up-to-date at least weekly, and agreed with suppliers' statements at least monthly. As far as possible, pay against statements — not against invoices.

VAT

Unless your sales are below the VAT threshold you need to charge VAT to your customers and pay it quarterly to H.M. Customs & Excise. Your cash book or sales journal should be analysed to identify the VAT content of your sales. Likewise, the VAT charged to you on virtually all your purchases, and expenses, should be identified in your cash book and your purchase journal, so as it can be deducted from your quarterly settlement. VAT returns are always looked on as a thing of dread! If, however, you keep your records up-to-date, your VAT return should take no longer than quarter-of-an-hour to produce — that's a challenge for you!

Tax

PAYE is more of a nuisance than a difficulty, but it is unavoidable. If you are paying just yourself and a mate, simply use the Inland Revenue standard forms for your pay records. If you employ half a dozen people, invest in a small multi-copy pay-roll system (Safeguard is the best in our view). If you are employing over twenty people, sub-contract the hassle to a local computer bureau — they are really not expensive for this sort of service.

Tax on the business will be based on your annual accounts, but make sure that your books and your filing are up-to-date so that the information your accountant may need is available without a major research programme being mounted.

The DHSS

National Insurance administration is part and parcel of the weekly or monthly payroll routine and tends to be dealt with very closely in conjunction with PAYE. The need for adequate personnel records and files has been underlined by the recent introduction of the Statutory Sick Pay scheme and you must now keep proper records for all your employees.

So that is what you *have* to do. Now let us look at what you *should* do. There is far more to keeping control than having a minimum level of up-to-date financial books and records. They will, to a large extent, tell you where you are, but what they will not tell you is where you should have been, nor will they tell you where you have been, nor will they tell you where you are going. You need internal controls for *your* benefit. Let us examine the headings one by one:

Stock
No 'outside' influence requires you to introduce stock control. Many businesses, of course, do not carry stock, and in other cases the stock level is so small that any form of records would be a waste of time and money. Remember, however, our friends David and John, and their kitchen furniture business. One of the reasons they were going to need much more money than they had originally anticipated was the fact that their stock of raw materials and furniture would be building up to quite a high level in early months. In this sort of business it is just as important to know the stockholding as it is to have the bank balance, or a list of the debtors and creditors outstanding. Many a business has failed through too much stock, and therefore too little readily available cash.

Costing
This is another area which is vital for the running of any business, involved with manufacture or service. The price you charge your customer may not necessarily be based on your cost. A pricing policy based on 'what the market will stand' is not to be sneezed at. Having said that, you must know what your costs are — there is little point in accepting an order for anything unless the profit margin is there.

Performance

So if you have an adequate and sensible set of books and records, what should you be doing with them? How can you use them to tell you what you need to know? Basically you should be able to use them to provide you with a performance record to measure what you have achieved, what is currently happening and to enable you to plan ahead. Adequate records of this sort will enable you to avoid disasters and enable you to react positively when an opportunity presents itself.

We believe that every business should produce a profit plan at least annually and prepare monthly management accounts within two or three weeks of the end of each month. Monthly management accounts consist of at least a trading statement and a balance sheet. The trading statement should follow the same basic format as your profit plan, but instead of forecasting, you plot the actual figures each month. These, of course, should be compared with the profit plan to see if you are meeting your targets. The balance sheet is a statement of the assets and liabilities of your business at that particular time, and it is again important that the figures should be measured against what you expected the position to be.

At the beginning of this chapter we talked about effective control being a combination of systems, people and attitude. If you are starting your business on your own, from scratch, you open the post, sign the cheques, do everything, and know everything, about your business. In two years time however you may be employing forty people, and it is then you are really in danger of losing control. You have to know what is going on:

How many enquiries did you receive last week?
How many orders did you get last week?
How much does Bloggs & Co. owe you?
What is the size of your overdraft?
What sort of profit did you make on the French contract?
How much are you paying for your latest batch of raw material? Why?
What happened to the enquiry you had from France last month?
Why are the transport costs higher this month than last?

It goes on and on and on . . . but you need it all.

An efficiently-run, well-controlled company benefits externally and internally. Even if your contract price is a little higher than your competitors', you are likely to be awarded the contract, if your customers can rely on prompt efficient service and good documentation. Similarly, if your staff can see that you are efficient, then they tend to become so too. Stringent stock control must result in less staff pilferage — it has to be true.

So at all times keep control — the more successful you are, the more vulnerable you are. The more you prosper, the more reliant you become on other people, and the more remote you become from the action. So be prepared — however small your business, set up the controls now. They will stand you in good stead when you reach that first million!

17. How to beat the bureaucrats

The bureaucrats . . . that splendid body of men who labour on behalf of Her Majesty's Government, the nationalised industries and those of similar inclinations.

The best way to beat the bureaucrats . . . is to join them. It is a pity that they have such a terrible reputation — bound hand and foot by red tape, narrow minded, inefficient, capable of driving strong men to drink and, of course, the popular misconception that all VAT men and their like have bolts through their necks!

We would like to advise you that this is not true. Bureaucrats are human beings — admittedly some more so than others — but all are *definitely* human.

Seriously though, such people as the Inspector of Taxes, the VAT man, the D.H.S.S. and so on are becoming more helpful and increasingly aware of their need to aid the small businessman. There was a time when any form of officialdom was unapproachable on a personal level. If you rang up a Government body and asked someone's name you were merely quoted an extension number. All that is a thing of the past. If you need help or advice from any Government Department these days, you can go and see them or they will come and see you.

What is the point of asking your accountant to explain the PAYE system to you when you can learn it direct from the 'horse's mouth'? If you are just about to set up in business and take on a couple of staff, but do not understand anything about PAYE, go along to the local Inspector of Taxes office. Someone there will actually be pleased to help you. Again, if you want to know about VAT someone from the local office will come and visit you and will be pleased to be asked. Similarly if you need to know whether you can obtain commercial use on a property, you do not need to consult an architect. Go direct to your local planning officer and ask him. The big advantage of the bureaucrats is that they are *free*!

The message for this chapter is short and sweet. The bureaucrats are there to help so use their services as much as you possibly can. Make friends with them but do be careful not to fall foul of them — they do have awfully long memories. It is probably something to do with their legendary filing systems!

One piece of advice on the other side of the coin. If you find yourself locked in mortal combat with officialdom of any sort, and you know you are in the right, you do have a secret weapon — your local newspaper. For some reason bureaucracy has a horror of publicity. If you are absolutely sure of your facts, threatening an exposé of the situation is usually enough to break the deadlock. If you have to go so far as having your story published, our experience is that heaven and earth will be moved just to shut you up — in other words, you win!

Here is a case history to illustrate this point. I (Deborah) ran a small business in an old Cotswold farmhouse for a number of years. The planning authorities were very kind and turned a blind eye until business started to expand and it reached a point where I really did need new premises. I had to wait three months for the completion of a new industrial site in our local market town and the planners were quite happy to wait for me to move. They did stress however that if I was not out of the farmhouse by the end of three months they would have to take action to terminate my business activities there.

As the industrial site neared completion, I contacted all the usual services for connection, including Telecom, only to be told that I could not have a telephone installed for eighteen months. What applied to me, applied to the whole industrial estate. For my business, a telephone was absolutely essential since it was one of our main methods of obtaining orders. I ranted and raved, took it as high as I could — right up to regional level. No use, they would not budge. I talked to one or two of the other tenants who were renting space on the site. They were mostly light industrial companies and although the lack of telephone was inconvenient, it was not fundamental to their business.

With the threat of action from the Planning Authority hanging over my head, I took the whole story to our local newspaper. They printed it with great glee along the lines that bureaucracy was killing a good, profitable local industry. Magic — within ten days, I had not one telephone line, but two, and so did every other business on the site!

That is an extreme example. Remember you and the bureaucrats are going to be good buddies!

18. How to collect money and keep your customers happy

It is said that even in a domestic environment, money causes more problems than sex. Usually the troubles arise from misunderstanding. As a nation we are notoriously bad at talking about, and dealing with, money. We find it embarrassing and somehow not quite respectable. To succeed in business you have got to put these feelings behind you and bear in mind that you will not upset your customer in pressing for payment if from the very beginning of your relationship you have made your terms of payment absolutely clear.

We have set out below a seven point plan which we recommend you follow carefully.

Terms

Most customers want credit but for goodness sake do not give it to them unless you have to! Remember, the best way to aid the building of your business is to delay paying your bills as long as you can and obtain quick settlement from your customers, thus greatly reducing the amount of working capital you need.

If you are to grant credit terms, it is not unreasonable, and is fairly standard practice, to ask your customer to settle in full the value of the first order at the time of placing it. This will give you time to take up references and establish account facilities. You may think this a bit cheeky, particularly when dealing with large companies. Our experience is the larger the company, the less worried they seem to be about your needing to establish their credit worthiness.

Although they do vary from industry to industry, normal credit terms are 30 days from supply of goods or services. We strongly recommend you not to offer any more — you cannot afford it.

Having established the basis on which you may be willing to give your customer credit you should then take up references.

References

You should ask for a banker's reference and two trade references. In the case of the banker's reference you should ask your own bank to check this out for you. If you are in a hurry because a great deal of money (to you) is at stake, you can ask your bank to telephone your customer's bank. So far as the trade references are concerned, we suggest that you telephone rather than write to the companies quoted. If you write you will receive a standard letter back, painting as good a picture as possible about your prospective customer. Instead, ring up the sales ledger department of the company. Ask if the customer settles his account regularly and on time without argument, or does he require constant chasing. Be chatty, friendly and make sure that the person at the other end realises you are a small business and cannot afford to lose your money. This way he is more likely to confide his doubts to you.

Having acquired your references only you can really decide whether to proceed with credit terms. It is a risk you have to weigh up against the implications of losing your money. As a general rule we believe you should never never deal with a company who cannot obtain a banker's reference.

Invoicing

You cannot expect to be efficiently paid if you cannot efficiently invoice. Make sure your invoice goes out immediately the goods or service have been supplied. It is terribly important for speedy payment that the invoice is properly addressed and this applies particularly when you are supplying large organisations. Your invoice should be headed with the order number or contract number you have been given and the name of the project. Where you are dealing with an individual within the company, it is advisable to mark the invoice for his attention, since instantly he will be in a position to verify it.

Making friends with the right person

In most companies your invoice will first be passed to a director or senior manager for authorisation and it will then be passed down to the accounts department where the purchase ledger clerk will have responsibility for entering it in the books and producing a cheque for signature. You must get to know that purchase ledger clerk. When dealing with big companies particularly, you may be told initially that you cannot have your cheque because it is in the computer system and the computer will not be producing cheques for, say, ten days. This may well be true but even in the largest organisations the system can always be by-passed. Cheques can be produced by hand and often are. By making friends with the right person he or she can help you achieve this. Remember . . . big companies need small companies, they need your flexibility and service. Do not be intimidated about chasing your payment — it is your right so to do.

Chasing payment

So you have issued your invoice, to the right person, with the right information. Thirty days have elapsed and you have received no payment. Ring your friend, the purchase ledger clerk. Be kind, but firm, do not be afraid of pleading poverty — it is probably true! Make a note on the file of who you spoke to and on what date and then ring every two or three days thereafter until you receive payment. From experience we find that a standard letter chasing payments is ignored. Wearing down the opposition by friendly but constant telephone calls usually works like magic! Discipline yourself — either you, or someone in your office, should have sole responsibility for ensuring that as each payment falls due, a telephone call is made and recorded and that subsequent telephone calls are made on a regular basis until payment is received. On the whole it is better that whoever chases for money is not normally the person who sells to your customer. It is preferable for obvious reasons that the two functions are kept completely separate, though, of course this may not be possible in a small business.

Late payments

In our view an invoice is seriously overdue if the customer is over two weeks late in paying. It is then that you have to start applying the pressure. Still be polite, friendly and understanding, but absolutely adamant that payment must be made. At this point one or two things will happen. In by far the majority of cases you will simply receive your cheque but you should remember for the future that this customer has a tendency to be late in paying and therefore you should start chasing earlier and more firmly next time. The second possibility is that they are having difficulty in making the payment and signs you should look for usually 'stand out a mile'. First, the person you normally speak to will not be in and will not return your call. You will have a great deal of difficulty in getting hold of anyone. Second, when you do speak to someone they will have a milliard of excuses — there is no-one to sign the cheque, their accountant is not in until next week, payments are only made on the 15th of every month and the really tell-tale sign — they will advise you the cheque is in the post, but it will not turn up. Once your customer starts lying, you have got trouble. The moment you get these sort of signs threaten legal proceedings. A 'seven days or else' letter from your solicitors will probably produce results, but if a cheque is not immediately forthcoming, issue a writ.

Legal Proceedings

Any advice we give on legal proceedings should be prefaced by saying that they are not cheap. You need to weigh up the amount of the debt against the costs. Although if your claim for payment is upheld by the

Court, your customer will have to pay the costs, you would not be issuing a writ at all unless you were worried about their financial standing. You need to bear in mind that before you can get your money, your customer may well have gone bust. It's a balancing act. Your solicitor will issue the writ for you and will advise you as to what it will cost, and at what stages. Make sure that you give him the correct information. If, for example, the writ is issued in the incorrect name, your customer can have the whole matter set aside and require the writ to be reissued. This could lose you, and gain him, a couple of valuable weeks. Before finally issuing the writ always advise your customer at the highest possible level that it is with enormous regret that you are taking this step, thus giving him one last chance. If there is no response, go ahead.

In our view if you receive no payment before you obtain judgment for the writ, you are dealing with a very sick company indeed. Once judgment has been made, it is the job of the Court Sheriff or Bailiff to collect the money. This he may very well be able to do, but here again in some instances he may not succeed. In which case, if the sum of money outstanding is large enough (£1,000 + in our view) use the ultimate weapon — the Winding Up Order against the company. Every company, regardless of the seriousness of its financial state, will avoid at all costs the Winding Up Order. If granted, this enables you to appoint a Liquidator to dispose of their assets.

We would like to stress that most of these gruesome steps will not be necessary for you to take, but in our experience of dealing with companies in a serious financial position — he who shouts loudest gets paid.

Most people are really quite nice — when chasing payment do not be rude, abusive or threatening. You are much more likely to obtain payment by being firm but always polite, understanding and sympathetic to the other's problems. If your debtor lives close at hand, a personal visit usually works wonders. Nine times out of ten you will leave with a cheque.

Remember too that payment does not have to be all or nothing. If your customer is finding things a little difficult, suggest instalment payments and be prepared to be flexible on these if you can. Remember you will gain nothing by putting him out of business.

If you deal with slow payers on a regular basis you need to be quite clear in your own mind whether they are slow payers because of administrative or financial problems. If it is financial be wary, do not start next month's work until they have paid for last, or try and devise a scheme whereby they can pay you regular instalment payments. If it is purely administrative, you may well be able to short-circuit this by the methods already suggested. If not, bear in mind that your money anywhere but in your bank 'costs'. If you have a good customer who persistently takes three months to pay, you must build the interest factor into the cost of your goods or services and do not be afraid to tell him so. He then has a choice to pay you promptly or pay you for the use of your money.

So . . . be efficient, be firm and be on your guard — you know how hard it is to get a sale — you cannot afford not to be paid for it.

Case History

One of our associate companies in the exhibition trade has a very large customer — in fact a well-known public company. Last year, for the first time, the public company did not settle its account on time following an exhibition. After a few days of normal chasing by the accounts department the matter was brought to the attention of the Managing Director because a substantial sum was involved (equivalent to the whole of one year's profit). The Managing Director was astounded. He could not believe there was any serious problem and in any event the company in question was one of his major customers. Competition is always high for their contract and it would be very easy to lose it. He began chasing for payment at a high level and within only a week received all the tell-tale signs of promises not kept. So, with a sinking heart he issued a writ. It produced an immediate response and payment in full, by instalments, over a couple of months.

The story has a happy ending. The public company was indeed in trouble but it survived and has placed its order for this year with our colleague again. Did he panic unnecessarily? When one considers that his action could have cost his company one of their biggest customers? After all, it was a public company of some standing. Is it possible to justify his actions? The answer is yes, yes a million times yes. If he had not reacted to the signs, the public company had not survived and had not paid up, then our colleague would have lost his company too. The size of the debt was too great a sum to gamble.

Remember it's the jungle you are in — survival is the primary law.

19. How to owe money and keep your creditors happy

Creditors' money in your business is the cheapest form of finance. By that, we do not mean that you should run up big debts and make commitments you cannot honour, but clever handling of your payments can be an extremely profitable exercise.

When you start a new business it is always difficult to obtain credit from suppliers. You are in a 'chicken and egg' situation — your suppliers will give you credit when you have a track record and you can only obtain a track record when somebody gives you credit. When applying to a supplier for credit terms, avoid if at all possible mentioning you are a new business unless asked the direct question. If a supplier insists on cash with order or cash on delivery, agree to it, but for a limited period only. For example, agree to pay cash for two consignments and thereafter expect normal monthly terms.

In most industries normal monthly terms are thirty days credit from the date of invoice. If however you can negotiate with your suppliers sixty or ninety days it can make a tremendous difference to your cash flow. Look carefully at your major suppliers and plot the impact of an extra month's credit — you will be amazed. Try a little gentle persuasion. If you are dealing with a big company an extra thirty days credit will be of little significance to them. The impact on your business, however, could be substantial. Using creditors' money, which is free, is infinitely preferable to using bank money . . . which costs!

The golden rule in the establishment of your business is to pay on time. Whether it is cash on the nail or credit terms, pay up on time — this is the only way to establish a credit rating. You must build up a good reputation. Once you are known to be a poor payer within your trade it is a very difficult reputation to reverse.

A few practical hints on paying suppliers. Once you have started to build a reputation for paying promptly, you can start taking advantage of your suppliers' inefficiency. Only pay suppliers who actually ask for their money. In other words, if a supplier is too easy-going or inefficient to send you a statement at the end of the month, do not feel worried about paying him late. As a general rule always insist on a statement — do not pay against an invoice. If a supplier asks you for less than you think you owe, pay the lesser amount. Let him find his mistake. On the other hand, if a supplier is asking for more than you think you owe, still pay him the lesser amount. Always assume that your accounts are more accurate and up-to-date than your suppliers'. Check off suppliers' statements very carefully against your records. It is so easy to overpay if you are settling individual invoices and not paying against agreed statements.

It is surprising just how inefficient suppliers can be about chasing their money. We were talking to the accountant of a very reputable firm the other day and he told us that currently he has on his books something over £20,000 of unclaimed money which is quite genuinely due to suppliers. This will eventually be paid over as and when the suppliers realise their mistakes, but in the meantime his company will have had the use of the money. We are not encouraging you to be dishonest but there is no harm in taking advantage of the inefficiency of others.

Good Cash Flow?

If, as your business grows, you find you are flush with cash, remember that taking cash discount is the easiest way of making profit. In these circumstances negotiate with your major suppliers — ask for a discount for settling on time. Ask for a bigger discount for settling in 7 days or on receipt of goods. Ask for an even bigger discount for cash with order, but here be careful. You should only do this if you completely trust the quality and performance of your supplier.

Cash Flow Problems?

Practically every business suffers from this at some stage. Owing money you cannot pay is awful. It is terrifying. It saps your confidence and the immediate understandable reaction is to bury one's head in the sand — anything but face up to the problem.

You must avoid this at all costs. If you find that it is going to be difficult to meet your commitments on time, preferably tell your supplier you cannot pay him on the due date before he starts chasing you — and what applies to suppliers equally well applies to PAYE, the VAT man, reduction of bank overdraft, or whatever. This underlines the need for good record keeping as detailed in Chapter 16. If you know where you are going you can see a financial hiccup ahead and cope with it.

If you are being chased for money do not run away. There is nothing that will aggravate a supplier more than if you do not answer his letters or telephone calls — apart from anything else, it is rude. Explain carefully your position and ask for extra time to pay. Payments by instalment are usually best. Few suppliers like the idea of receiving nothing from you. Regular payments for a fairly extended period are usually quite acceptable if you are able to convince your supplier that you have a basically viable business. Remember it becomes increasingly more difficult to negotiate terms the further down the legal slippery slope you slide. It is relatively easy to negotiate with a supplier, it is far more difficult to negotiate with his solicitor and extremely difficult to negotiate with the bailiff! Avoid at all costs the debt going into legal hands. Once that happens you are stuck on the 'merry-go-round' and it is difficult to get off.

If things are looking very black indeed, do not despair. It is in nobody's interest to close you down or make you bankrupt and most people realise this. The best way of getting their money back is to see you stay in business. Provided *you* are convinced that given time your cash flow problems can be controlled, then in our view you will be able to convince your creditors as well.

Credit is dangerous. We all know that from our monthly credit card statements! Why is it that we have always spent more than we thought we had? Do not take any more credit than you can afford and build up good relationships with your suppliers — they are quite as valuable to you as your backers and bankers.

Case History

We have a shareholding in a little advertising agency. In its first year of trading it had done remarkably well. It had built up a list of regular clients but one in particular — a very old established company (a household name) — was responsible for about half of the agency's business.

One Friday night we had a panic call from the Managing Director of the agency. His major client was in trouble and he was owed tens of thousands of pounds. After a worried weekend, we took decisive action and on Monday morning served a writ on his client. Unfortunately it was too late. A Receiver had been appointed and it became immediately apparent that there was no question of anyone collecting their debts. On the face of it our advertising agency was finished.

We talked the matter through all morning. No bank was going to lend us more money simply to finance a bad debt. From the agency's point of view it was a double blow. Not only had they lost a great deal of money, but they had also lost their major client. In these circumstances they could not possibly generate new sales fast enough to put sufficient money back into the company to pay their own creditors.

The Managing Director did the only thing he could. He personally went round to each of his suppliers and explained the position. What he asked them to do was to write off their profit on all the money he owed and to give him extended credit to repay the balance. By the end of the day he had reduced the money he owed by £12,000. Yes his suppliers had lost their profit but they kept their customer in business. It was an investment for the future. Even the VAT man accepted settlement over a six-month period.

Now nearly a year later the agency is really flourishing. It has finished paying back all the old debts and has found new clients. At the end of the day it was the Managing Director's reputation for honesty and integrity that won through. He had always played fair with his suppliers and therefore when things became tough, they were more than happy to reciprocate.

20. How to be a successful opportunist

A successful business is all about seizing opportunities. In this section of our book we have spent a considerable amount of time telling you about the importance of having controls, plans, budgets and forecasts; of being cautious and prudent. But you would not be going into business at all if you were not an opportunist — if you had not seen an opening of which to take advantage.

After that initial decision to start your own business, opportunities will continue to present themselves from time to time. Back the right ones and your business will grow — back a loser and you will be in trouble. Opportunism in the context of a plan is good. Unplanned opportunism results in over-trading. Over-trading often results in bankruptcy. Opportunities present themselves usually in one of two ways. Either you have the chance to make a big purchase or a big sale.

Purchasing

It may be that you have the opportunity, as a manufacturer, to buy a large quantity of raw material at an especially good price. It may be that you have the chance to buy in bulk a product on which you feel you can make a tremendous profit. Either way, you need to weigh up the pros and cons. This huge quantity of raw material. How long is it going to last you with your current production output — six months — a year — more? Will it deteriorate? Will it become out of date? Equally relevant, if you are going to have to borrow money to make such a big purchase, what happens to that wonderful bargain price when you have added on the interest you will be charged? If it is a finished product you are buying, is it something you handle in the normal course of business? For example, just because you have a garden centre, do you necessarily want to buy 10,000 plastic gnomes without first proving to yourself that your customers want such things. The gnomes may be cheap, but they suddenly become awfully expensive if they are stock you cannot sell.

The third form of big purchase that may come your way is a development opportunity. This could take the form of a chance to buy new premises, new equipment — even the opportunity to take on a highly qualified member of staff. You need to weigh up what you will lose by letting the opportunity go by, against what you will lose if your commitment is too great.

Selling

This is a problem which often besets the small and new business. You are plodding along, just eaking out a living from supplying one or two customers on a regular basis, when *wham*! Out of nowhere, comes the opportunity to undertake a really large contract which will put you 'on the map'. Of course you must do it, but you would be surprised how many businesses go to the wall in just these circumstances. They simply bite off more than they can chew.

So whether you are buying or selling, if it is on a scale outside the pattern of normal trading, you must plan. Work out exactly how much space you need, how many extra people you must have, how much extra equipment will be required. You will need additional finance. Work out your costings (be pessimistic) and take the scheme to your backer or banker. As we have said, businesses are built on seizing opportunities. If your scheme is a sound one, you will not be turned down.

Perhaps the most important ingredient in business development is timing. Before plunging ahead, make sure you have really done your research. What is the life span of this new product. Are you going to be able to sell it in a year's time? This huge order you are getting, is it a 'one-off'? When you have finished it, will you find yourself with extra staff and extra machinery, which you will not need on a day-to-day basis?

Take a craze like skate boarding. A few people made a great deal of money. They saw the craze coming and they anticipated its decline. They got out in time. But for every one of those, there were many people who lost fortunes. In hindsight, it was obviously foolish to sink long-term money into a kids' passing fashion.

A colleague of ours has a lovely story. He has a very successful business, but cannot resist the extra odd deal here and there. Some years ago, he was given the opportunity of importing into this country, several hundred thousand chocolate Father Christmases. They were a marvellous bargain and he was destined to make about 300% profit on the deal. Fantastic. Everything went like a dream, except that the Father Christmases arrived at the docks on January 3rd! As he said: 'Have you ever tried selling a chocolate Father Christmas in January?'

If you are going to start wheeling and dealing, pay very strict attention to detail, and make sure your risk is containable. What happens if the deal goes wrong? The risk must not be so great that it can ruin your business. The chocolate Father Christmas saga was embarrassing and costly, but there was no question of it ruining our friend's business.

But do not let us dampen your ardour. Keep your eyes open and your wits about you, and if you are sure you are on to something, stick with it. Take the example of Sir Terence Conran and Habitat. Modern furniture twenty years ago was unbelievably dull. He knew it and set about designing and making a whole new concept in furniture, but he could not sell it. Stores just did not want to know. What did he do — pack up and abandon the idea? No, he knew he was right so he opened his own shop and the rest, as they say . . . is history.

132

'The Consequences'

In today's difficult financial climate, you need to recognise that you may well fail, however careful you are.

Yet sufficiently volatile is the world of commerce, that you may equally find you have created a Monster . . .

21. Failure

It *is* possible to fail successfully.

The reasons for business failure are diverse and complex. Sometimes failure is unavoidable, though more often it is a combination of bad luck and bad judgement. The Famous Five causes of business failure are:

(1) Underestimating the cash required to run the business, just like Bernard, our Case History No. 2 in Chapter 9.

(2) A combination of poor market research and bad analysis of sales, resulting in large stocks of slow moving items.

(3) Lack of sales drive, like our friend in Case History No. 2 in Chapter 5.

(4) Poor costings — the common misconception is that high turnover

means high profit. The inability to accurately gauge gross profit margins to ensure that they cover the overheads.

(5) People reasons — incompatability of partners, or the wrong staff in the wrong job — like Barbara and Elizabeth in Case History No. 2 in Chapter 7, or Peter from Birmingham, Case History No. 1 in Chapter 12.

Most businesses fail through a combination of the above in varying degrees, and once a business starts heading in a downward spiral, it is amazing how quickly it can collapse.

It is at this point that you can turn failure into success. When your business hits a difficult patch, the first stage of being able to do something about it is to recognise it is happening. (Sorry to harp on again here, but good controls and proper management accounts will ensure that this is the case). Having recognised the problem, somehow, and goodness knows it is not easy, you need to stand back, look at your business and ask yourself honestly whether you believe you can trade out of trouble. Seek help and guidance from someone you trust, but as with starting a business, the decision to voluntarily pack up is yours and yours alone. To be faced with failure is a terrible thing — the hours — perhaps years — of struggle coming to nothing in the end. It is in these circumstances one is tempted to have one last try, one last desperate attempt to 'save the day'. However, if fail you must, the most painless way to do it is to fade out. The gradual wind down of a business very often means that no-one gets hurt, but the spectacular bankruptcies and liquidations you read about in the press, are so often caused by that one last push. One has to face it, why should your fourth sales drive work any better than the previous three just because you are that much more desperate?

While a business is a going concern you can obtain a better price for everything. If the business is not viable enough to sell, there is still the property, the equipment and the stock, which will all fetch a much better price if you are still trading. Also, and this is important, whilst you may feel that your business is worthless because you are on the verge of bankruptcy, it does not mean that it is not worth something to someone else. It is very easy to stand back and look at someone else's operation and think one could do better. Faced with failure, you are looking for a guy who thinks like that! We know a classic case of a restaurant not far from our home. The restaurant site has had four different proprietors and each one of them has gone bankrupt. Why? Well we do not know, but we suspect that there is something fundamentally wrong with the site. The interesting point is that there was nothing wrong with the four restauranteurs, except their pride. Each in turn thought the previous occupant had got it wrong and that they could do better — thank goodness the site has been turned into a block of flats now!

So the message for this chapter is to recognise when you are beat. Pull out slowly, carefully and with dignity, your primary concern being to protect your creditors, your backers . . . and yourself.

We have talked at length to a very experienced Receiver, who is a partner in a large firm of London Accountants. He was adamant that in his experience, it takes people at least two years to recover from the failure of their business. It is a very harrowing experience. So if you are faced with failure recognise that you are not at your best. Do not start dashing off on tangents, nor indeed make any major decisions immediately after the collapse. Do not panic, take time to think out your next move, even if you have to live on bread and dripping for a few weeks. It is when you are in this vulnerable state that you can heap mistake on mistake. And never forget the old adage, that it is better to have tried and failed than never to have tried at all.

22. Success

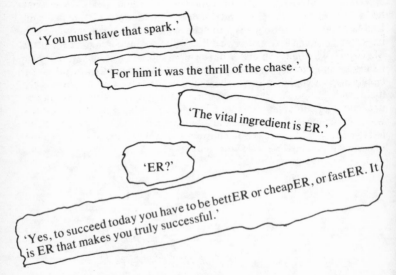

'You must have that spark.'

'For him it was the thrill of the chase.'

'The vital ingredient is ER.'

'ER?'

'Yes, to succeed today you have to be bettER or cheapER, or fastER. It is ER that makes you truly successful.'

As part of our research for this book we have talked to several people, who have achieved outstanding success in the business world. Not through luck, or inheritance, but through sheer ability and hard work. We wanted to pick their brains — was there a magic formula that we could pass on to you, our reader? The results were extraordinary. The people we interviewed were diverse in character. They came from different backgrounds, had different trades, different skills . . . but it was like interviewing one man. Let us explain what we mean.

Sir Maxwell Joseph is a supreme example of the entrepreneur achieving outstanding success. He is probably best known to the public for his hotel chain, Grand Metropolitan Hotels, though his empire stretched far beyond that and is immense. Sir Maxwell died last year, and we talked to his widow about his phenomenal achievements. What was the secret of his success? Lady Joseph felt that one of the main characteristics that helped him succeed was singlemindedness. She told the story of how each day he had delivered to the house every single national newspaper. He would rise at 5.30 a.m. and read them all before going to the office. But ask him what he thought about the Russians invading Afghanistan or the winners of the Cup Final and he would not know what you were talking about. His concentration on the financial and property press was so intense, he would never even notice the head-lines! Did immense wealth change him? No, not really, it seems, but for the fact that it enabled him to do what he wanted, rather than what he had to. And the spur — what drove him on? 'It was the chase,' said Lady Joseph, 'the thrill was in the chase. Money and power were not important. He just loved what he did.' We talked for some time about Sir Maxwell's views and beliefs. What clearly emerged was that he did what he did because he enjoyed it. The fact that he was so good at it that he became one of the country's richest and most powerful men, was purely incidental. What emerged was the profile of a rather nice, quiet, unassuming family man, who loved his job. Sir Maxwell Joseph's story was comforting, but we felt he must be the exception. We have all been led to believe that success and enormous wealth almost always go hand in hand with unhappiness and discontent.

From Lady Joseph, we went to see a Czechoslovakian businessman, who had built a fortune in the leather business. He showed us into his office and there began the story of his life. He arrived in the U.K. in 1939, aged fifteen, and a refugee. At Victoria Station he had to borrow the taxi fare to take him to his digs, yet ten years later he had a well-established slipper factory, turning over hundreds of thousands of pounds. Our Czechoslovakian was flamboyant and charming, but slowly, now familiar characteristics started to emerge. He loved his business — it was far more important to him than the trappings of wealth. His business was his job, his hobby, his life. One felt that like Sir Maxwell, he would be wheeling and dealing until the day he died.

So what do we learn from these great businessmen? We learn that dedication is essential. Their early struggles tell us of the need for hard work, their deals indicate the need for flair and imagination, but the essential ingredient for being successful is to enjoy what you do. Draw an analogy from your own childhood. What subjects were easiest for you at school? In what subjects did you obtain the best exam results? Think about it — they were the subjects you *liked* best.

Success is relative. It is good to see your hard work turned into solid achievement, to see money pile up in your bank account, but is it giving you and your family pleasure? Can financial gain at the expense of personal happiness be called 'success'. A colleague of ours, himself an extremely successful businessman, summed it up for us.

SUCCESS IS DIFFICULT TO ACHIEVE, MORE DIFFICULT TO SUSTAIN, AND EVEN MORE DIFFICULT TO ENJOY.

So from your first day in business to your last, get your priorities right. Enjoy it — life's too short to do anything else.

NOTES

NOTES

NOTES

NOTES

NOTES

NOTES

NOTES

NOTES